The
OVERCOMING
LIFE

RICK JOYNER

The
OVERCOMING
LIFE

RICK JOYNER

MorningStar Publications
A DIVISION OF MORNINGSTAR FELLOWSHIP CHURCH
375 Star Light Drive, Fort Mill, SC 29715

The Overcoming Life
by Rick Joyner
Copyright © 2006
2nd Printing, 2007

Distributed by MorningStar Publications, Inc.,
a division of MorningStar Fellowship Church
375 Star Light Drive, Fort Mill, SC 29715

International Standard Book Number: 1-59933-035-0; 978-1-59933-035-8

Cover Design: Kevin Lepp
Book Layout: Dana Zondory

MorningStar's website: www.morningstarministries.org
For information call 1-800-542-0278.

CONTENTS

PART II • 137
THE FRUIT OF THE SPIRIT

Part I

The Life That Will Last Forever

Creating a Clean Heart

CHAPTER ONE
THE HIGHEST CALLING

True Christianity is not a life of working, but of becoming. It is the pursuit of seeing the glory of the Lord and being changed by that glory into His same image. The true quest of the Christian life is to become like Christ and to do the works that He did with the same heart, being one with Him.

I recently heard a Christian businessman say that he felt the greatest mistake of Christianity has been to worship Jesus in place of becoming one with Him. Of course, this does not mean that we should not worship Jesus, but there is merit to the fact that many worship Him, instead of seeking union with Him. This book is about how to become united with Him, become like Him, and do the works that He did.

The Great Ingathering

Christians who live in these times have been chosen to be laborers in the greatest harvest the world has ever known. In the last two decades, we have witnessed the greatest advance of Christianity in history. Whole continents are now being transformed by the gospel. More people have become Christians since 1985 than have from the beginning of the church age in the first-century until now, and the pace is increasing. As the Lord said, **"the harvest is the end of the age" (see Matthew 13:39)**. Certainly, this is the greatest time of harvest the world has ever seen. However, the "Great Commission" is about more than just making converts, it is the call to "make disciples."

The Great Commission is about raising up Christians with depth, character, and power. That is what this book is about—the ultimate quest of the true Christian life which is much more than just acknowledging certain doctrines—it is the devotion to **"...speaking the truth in love, we are to grow up in all aspects into Him, who is the head, even Christ" (Ephesians 4:15)**. **"All aspects"** means being like Him and doing the works that He did.

In His life on the earth, Jesus demonstrated authority over all of the conditions on the earth. We are called to do the same. However, before we can be trusted with the miraculous power to change the conditions on earth, we must be changed and have authority over all of the conditions in our own personal lives. This is a step-by-step, systematic growth and maturity, which is summarized as walking in "the fruit of the Spirit."

Fruit does not just happen—it is grown. This takes planting, watering, cultivating, protecting, and not the least of all—time. When people are born, they are just starting their lives, and when they are born-again, they are likewise just starting their spiritual lives. As the Lord also said concerning these times in Matthew 24:19, **"But woe to those who are with child and to those who nurse babes in those days!"** I would interpret this as: "Woe to those who keep their people in immaturity!" The true measure of Christian maturity is the fruit of the Spirit. This book is about how we grow that fruit.

Some may recoil at the thought that we must grow this fruit. Is it not the fruit of the Spirit? Yes, but we have a part to play in cultivating and growing the fruit of the Spirit. We cannot do it without the Spirit, but neither can the Spirit grow it without us.

I once heard a story about how a farmer had asked his pastor to come home with him for Sunday lunch. As his wife was preparing the meal, the farmer was showing his pastor around and remarked about the beautiful crops he was growing. The pastor corrected him and said, "You didn't grow those crops. God did." The farmer looked at him kind of funny and then said, "Yes, that's true, but I helped. In fact, let me show you the field that I let God grow all by Himself!"

There is an important truth to this story. Just as the Lord put man in the Garden of Eden to cultivate it, the Lord created man to be a crucial part of His work. The same is true of the fruit of the Spirit. There is no question that it is, in fact, the "fruit of the Spirit," and cannot be accomplished without the Holy Spirit, but it also requires our contribution and cooperation.

Just as it was a great joy for the Lord to walk with man in the Garden, and certainly this had to be the greatest joy for Adam, there is a special fellowship with God that we can have in this work of cultivating, which is a great joy to God and can also be our greatest joy. As one study recently pointed out, the number one question that people had was what their purpose was. To the degree that we know and are engaged in our purpose, we will have peace and fulfillment in this life. Until we know it and are engaged in it, we will only know discord and anxiety.

For this reason, what we are about to address in this book may be the most important matter of all for our own health and well-being. This will lead to the most exciting and fulfilling life that can be experienced on this earth, but even more important than that, it is about pleasing and serving our Maker. He deserves this devotion, and through it we will learn more about Him and can observe the most exciting and fulfilling events we can know in this life—the activity of God that reveals His ways.

Just as a farmer or gardener has much joy in watching the seeds sprout and grow until the fruit appears, as Christians we should have this same joy as the fruit of the Spirit grows in our lives, and we are then able to be used to spread the seeds and help cultivate them in others. This is the basis for authentic Christianity.

Going Under the Knife

We are living in the time when the church is preparing to cross its Jordan River and start possessing its Promised Land. We are seeing many of the great prophetic promises of Scripture fulfilled in our time. To understand this, we are told to observe these events in Israel's history and understand that they are prophetic parallels. As we are told in I Corinthians 10, after rehearsing the events of Israel's journey in the wilderness, the apostle writes in verse 11, **"Now these things happened to them as an example, and they were written for our instruction, upon whom the ends of the ages have come."**

We will follow the same pattern that they did in possessing our promises. It is therefore important for us to understand when Israel began to eat the fruit of the land after they had crossed over, which is recorded in Joshua 5:8-12:

> **Now it came about when they had finished circumcising all the nation, that they remained in their places in the camp until they were healed.**
>
> **Then the Lord said to Joshua, "Today I have rolled away the reproach of Egypt from you." So the name of that place is called Gilgal to this day.**
>
> **While the sons of Israel camped at Gilgal, they observed the Passover on the**

evening of the fourteenth day of the month on the desert plains of Jericho.

And on the day after the Passover, on that very day, they ate some of the produce of the land, unleavened cakes and parched grain.

And the manna ceased on the day after they had eaten some of the produce of the land, so that the sons of Israel no longer had manna, but they ate some of the yield of the land of Canaan during that year.

After crossing the Jordan River, the people had to stop and circumcise all who had not been circumcised in the wilderness. Circumcision is a prophetic type of cutting away the flesh or the carnal nature. This had to be done, and then they had to celebrate the Passover Feast, which for us is a celebration of how "Christ, our Passover" delivered us from the bondage of this world. For us, this represents a re-emphasis of the cross and its work in our lives. For this reason, we can expect the cross and the crucified life to become a great emphasis of the church in the time to come. We can expect this to result in the exposure of carnal nature, or the deeds of the flesh from the life of the church, which is described in Galatians 5:19-21:

Now the deeds of the flesh are evident, which are: immorality, impurity, sensuality,

idolatry, sorcery, enmities, strife, jealousy, outbursts of anger, disputes, dissensions, factions,

**envying, drunkenness, carousing, and
things like these, of which I forewarn you just
as I have forewarned you that those who
practice such things shall not inherit the
kingdom of God.**

The children of Israel could not possess their
Promised Land until this was done. Just as Paul wrote
for Christians, **"those who practice such things shall
not inherit the kingdom of God."** Think about that!
We will not inherit the kingdom of God as long as we
practice these things. As the Word of God is also clear,
those who are indeed the Lord's will behave like it.
They are different. They have the fruit of the Spirit,
and they are devoted to living godly, righteous, holy
lives. Again, those who do not walk in this way will
not inherit the kingdom of God.

In our time, righteousness has often been asso-
ciated with legalism or even having a religious
spirit, but those who have overreacted to this have
usually fallen to another evil that is just as deadly—
lawlessness. There is a ditch on either side of the
path of life. If we live as reactionaries, we will likely
end up in one of them or going from one to the other
most of our lives. Now let's take a look at the spiritual
circumcision and how it is accomplished in our lives,
as we read in Romans 2:28-29, 7:18, 8:5-9:

**For he is not a Jew who is one out-
wardly; neither is circumcision that which
is outward in the flesh.**

But he is a Jew who is one inwardly; and circumcision is that which is of the heart, by the Spirit, not by the letter; and his praise is not from men, but from God.

For I know that nothing good dwells in me, that is, in my flesh; for the wishing is present in me, but the doing of the good is not.

For those who are according to the flesh set their minds on the things of the flesh, but those who are according to the Spirit, the things of the Spirit.

For the mind set on the flesh is death, but the mind set on the Spirit is life and peace,

because the mind set on the flesh is hostile toward God; for it does not subject itself to the law of God, for it is not even able to do so;

and those who are in the flesh cannot please God.

However, you are not in the flesh but in the Spirit, if indeed the Spirit of God dwells in you.

Recent studies have shown that those who claim to be born-again, evangelical Christians are no longer distinguishable from non-Christians in their general behavior, including basic issues of morality and integrity. This is why the heathen continue to refer to Christians as hypocrites. This cannot, and will not, continue.

Certainly, a good case could be made that in the church's wilderness journey there has not been much emphasis on the spiritual circumcision that is required if we are going to inherit our promises. However, we can count on this becoming a major emphasis in the immediate future. The true church will not go any further until the flesh, or the carnal nature, has been cut away from the lives of those who will inherit the kingdom.

Like it or not, the works of the flesh are going to be exposed and cut away from all who want to be numbered with the household of faith. It is noteworthy that for Israel this was the first thing which was done immediately after they had entered the land, and it was done right in the sight of the people on the walls of Jericho. This was not something the Lord did secretly in the wilderness; they were humiliated and made weak, right within sight of their enemies! Is this not what has been happening to the church in recent times?

One lesson we can learn from this is that the Lord is not nearly as concerned about our reputations as we tend to be. In fact, we can count on Him dealing with that pride very quickly. We think that if our problems are waved in front of the world we will lose our "witness," but the Lord cares very little about that. In fact, such a witness will not lead anyone to the Lord. The only things that will truly lead people to the Lord is the conviction of their sin by the Holy Spirit and the comprehension of the atonement that Jesus made for that sin. This is the only remedy for our guilt. It is about Him, not us. Preaching the gospel is about lifting Him up, not ourselves.

Then why are we devoting so much attention to growing the fruit of the Spirit in our lives? Because this is the way we were created to be. It is the reforming of the image of God in us. It is the work and proof of a truly redeemed life. His true disciples will be known by their love. The Father wants His family to love one another and to love their neighbors. As the Apostle Paul said in I Corinthians 13:1, **"If I speak with the tongues of men and of angels, but do not have love, I have become a noisy gong or a clanging cymbal."** We might paraphrase this: Without love Christians are just a lot of noise with no substance.

If we are indeed coming to the time when the body of Christ begins to truly possess and walk *in* its promises, we can expect the carnal problems of the church to be exposed openly until they are removed. We are going through a great spiritual circumcision right now. This is being done to bring these problems to the light so they can be removed. We can count on our enemies seeing this and rejoicing over it, but our humility in this is preparing us to be able to receive the grace of God, which He will only give to the humble.

The victory over our enemies will come in due time, but for now the best thing that we can do is embrace humility and let the evil ways that we have clung to be cut away.

For this reason, we will also use the beginning of this study to examine these works of the flesh in a bit more detail. This can be painful, but we can do some things that will greatly lessen the pain. As we are told in I Corinthians 11:31, **"But if we judged ourselves rightly, we should not be judged."** If we will deal with these things, the Lord will not have to do it. If we will humble ourselves, He will not have to humble us.

If there is a humility and submission in our hearts to the work of the Lord, this process will be much less painful than if we fight it. If we pursue an understanding of the works of the flesh and seek to discern any evil way that is in our own lives, this can actually be a much less painful journey than many make it out to be. It is far better for us to fall on the Rock and be broken than to have Him fall on us and crush us into powder! So, if we deal with these things ourselves, and if we judge ourselves, we can in fact escape the more painful and public humiliation.

Even so, there is a more righteous motivation that we should have, and hopefully will mature into. That is to do it for the Lord's sake—to do it in order to please Him. However, until the flesh or carnal nature is cut away, it is hard to have such godly motives. So, even if we do it out of the basically selfish motive of wanting to get out of this as easily as possible, or to advance ourselves in the kingdom, it is better to do it for these reasons than not doing it at all. As we mature, our motives will change. Even so, know for sure that it must be done before we can go any further. We can also know for sure that whatever pain we suffer will result in gain for us.

CHAPTER TWO
THE PATH OF LIFE

The Scriptures are clear that the wise love discipline and correction. I am assuming that only a Christian with a certain level of maturity would even care to read a book like this one, so we are going to go after some hard issues right up front. We will be dealing in some depth with the works of the flesh and the roots of evil strongholds, which will keep us in defeat and need to be broken in our lives. Then we will examine the fruit of the Spirit, the bearing of which should be an ultimate goal for every Christian and the true mark of Christian maturity.

A famous general who was pondering the poor condition of his troops reportedly remarked, "We have met the enemy and he is us!" One thing we need to settle now is that the devil does not cause us nearly as many problems as we cause ourselves. To be free of our worst enemy, the "body of death," which is our "old self," we must submit to the circumcision of the Holy Spirit who cuts away our carnal nature and kills our old self. The Lord is not just trying to change us—He is trying to kill us! He is trying to kill our old self so we can walk in resurrection life. However, we cannot be resurrected unless we have first died.

Christians have the highest calling and should have lives filled with the greatest vision and purpose of any who walk on the earth. We are called to be like Jesus! The Holy Spirit has been given to us to bring forth the nature of the Son of God in us. Christians do not follow gurus, because we have God Himself living in us in the Person of the Holy Spirit. Therefore, all Christians who are walking in the light should have every day filled with awe and wonder of God who is with us. As we are told in Proverbs 4:18-19:

But the path of the righteous is like the light of dawn, that shines brighter and brighter until the full day.

The way of the wicked is like darkness; they do not know over what they stumble.

The normal Christian life is one of increasing light. Our path should be getting brighter and brighter. Only the wicked walk in darkness and stumble over things they do not see. This includes Christians who have departed from the path of life to walk in ways of wickedness. The works of the flesh, which we are about to study, are the ways of wickedness that create darkness and the stumbling about that so many Christians are subject to. If we depart from these ways and return to the path of life, then our lives will get brighter and brighter until we are walking in the fullness of the light. Therefore, we will study these in some depth before going on to the works of light, the fruit of the Spirit.

We must have a positive vision of where we are going and what we are called to do, but we also need to understand that the fallen, carnal nature of man is in basic conflict with the Spirit and the purposes of God, and this must be removed in us before we will be of much use to our King. As discussed, in Scripture "the flesh" is a metaphor for the carnal nature of fallen man which is in opposition to the Spirit of God.

It is crucial that the deeds of the flesh: **"immorality, impurity, sensuality, idolatry, sorcery, enmities, strife, jealousy, outbursts of anger, disputes, dissensions, factions, envying, drunkenness, carousing, and things like these" (Galatians 5:19-21)** be overcome by Christians. We are told in Galatians 5:21, as long as we practice this carnal nature, we **"shall not inherit the kingdom of God."** That alone should be a most sobering challenge. This is not an option for Christians.

The removal of that nature is referred to as our spiritual circumcision, which is the circumcision of our hearts, as we read in Romans 2:27-29, in the first chapter of this book. We will take the time to look at each of these works of the flesh and how they are to be cut out of our lives. Next, we will examine how they are replaced by the fruit of the Spirit, which is the Christ-like nature. Our goal is not just to rid ourselves of the evil, but to fill our hearts with God.

The first work of the flesh that is listed is **"immorality."** This includes fornication, which is having sex outside of marriage, and adultery, which is having sex with someone other than your spouse when you, or they, are married. It also includes homosexual sex, which the Bible calls not only a sin, but a perversion and an abomination. These are sins and they are forbidden. Under no circumstance are they acceptable behavior for a Christian.

Does that mean that anyone who has ever fallen to one of these cannot inherit the kingdom of God? No, there is grace for those who stumble, if we repent and seek the forgiveness of God through His atonement. However, it is a different story for those who **"practice"** these things. That implies the continual, repeated sin that is not repented of.

A second question would be whether a Christian who falls into repeated affairs or lengthy affairs can be saved because they have practiced these things? This is a good question and one that is certainly worthy of examination. It is addressed in a number of Scriptures, but we will look at Hebrews 6:4-6:

> **For in the case of those who have once been enlightened and have tasted of the heavenly gift and have been made partakers of the Holy Spirit,**

> **and have tasted the good word of God and the powers of the age to come,**

and then have fallen away, it is impossible to renew them again to repentance, since they again crucify to themselves the Son of God, and put Him to open shame.

There is obviously a line that can be crossed where it becomes impossible to be renewed again to repentance. This also implies that if someone can still repent, they must not have crossed that line. The key is if they can still repent. Repentance is more than just feeling sorry for having committed the sin, and more than asking forgiveness—it means to renounce the sin and turn away from it, resolving not to do it again. So if someone can still repent, they can be forgiven and still inherit the kingdom of God. Hebrews 3:13 says:

But encourage one another day after day, as long as it is still called "Today," lest any one of you be hardened by the deceitfulness of sin.

Sin does harden the heart toward repentance and makes it harder to repent. Sin is also deceitful, and those who practice it often become so deceived that they no longer see it as sin, and therefore cannot repent of it.

The power of sin to deceive is remarkable; however, being deceived is no excuse. Deception is in fact the result of compromising the clear Word of God by disobeying Him. This is why the very first temptation of Satan in the Garden was to get the woman to believe that God did not really mean what He said. Once we start rationalizing the clear Word of God, deception and sin are inevitable.

As C.S. Lewis once wrote, when you take a wrong turn on the path of life and start down the wrong road, it will never turn into the right road. The only way to get back on the right road is to go back to where you missed the turn. This is called repentance. Sin will never become righteousness. It will never be okay.

There have been great transgressions illuminated in many significant leaders in our time, which have caused many to stumble. The church today has also had some of the greatest leaders since the first century, which we should acknowledge and appreciate. There are great problems in the church today, but there are also many more reasons for great hope.

Though we have had to deal with some very ugly things in the church, many times in church leaders, this should not shake our faith of there ultimately being a bride without spot or wrinkle. Our faith should be in God, not people—not even the greatest leaders. There were significant flaws which came out in even the greatest biblical heroes, and they are illuminated in Scripture so we can understand them, and hopefully, not fall to the same things. But even the greatest people are still flesh and blood, and our faith must not rest on them. If our faith is in God, we will never be disappointed or shaken by the failures of others.

As we take some time to examine the works of the flesh and what practicing them can lead to, keep in mind that we are going to get to the fruit of the Spirit and the great things that are right now going on in the church. We must also keep in mind Galatians 6:1,

"Brethren, even if a man is caught in any trespass, you who are spiritual, restore such a one in a spirit of gentleness; each one looking to yourself, lest you too be tempted." I would say that **"any trespass"** covers anything. For this reason, I do not believe in giving up on anyone. We must have as our goal the restoration of anyone who falls into any sin.

Galatians 6:1 also makes it clear that the truly spiritual are in the business of restoring others who have fallen into sin. Think about that. How many restoration ministries are there in the body of Christ? How many churches know how to restore their members who stumble? I have been around the world a number of times, visiting more countries than I care to count, and in every case, it was to visit the church there. Yet, I can only think of a handful of ministries in the world that give any attention to a true restoration ministry. It is certainly hard for the heathen to believe our message about redemption when we will not even help our own who fall instead of condemning them. This is also evidence of the tragic spiritual immaturity of the church.

As we read in Hebrews 6, there obviously is a line that can be crossed where it becomes impossible for one to repent. But until the Lord has revealed that this has clearly happened, it should be our resolve to help restore anyone from **"any trespass."** Regardless of how deep the darkness is that someone falls into, we should resolve to hope and pray for his repentance and do anything we can to help him as the Lord gives us the grace. Think of the deep depravity that the world has fallen into, yet the Lord has not given up on it. He will restore it to its originally intended purpose and state, as the Scriptures make very clear.

The Time to Run

In this study, I will share some of my own experiences and some of the things I have encountered in the church. I am not doing this for shock value or to just expose people, but for this reason: The Spirit in which the Scriptures were written exposed the failures of even its greatest heroes so others could learn from them and avoid them. I will not use names, unless it is with that person's permission. Some of them you may guess, but exposing people is not my intent. I know if we are going to receive mercy, we need to sow mercy every chance we get. If we are going to receive grace, we need to sow grace every chance we get. I hope you can understand that even the foulest things I share are for the sake of illuminating the deceitfulness of sin so that others may be delivered from it.

I once happened upon an entire movement that is very large and seemed to be helping a lot of people, especially the poor and oppressed. However, the leaders believed that the more anointed you were, the more concubines you needed, which is why they claimed King David and Solomon needed so many. The tragedy of the lives and families destroyed by this movement is now becoming public, but this is sadly not the end of the story. This same tragic delusion has crept into other movements. The Bible does not tell us to overcome immorality, but to flee from it. If you happen upon anything like this, do not hesitate to flee just as fast as you can!

Of course, this deceived movement claimed that only "the mature" could understand this kind of "revelation," so it was not taught openly. The level of immorality and perversion in this movement would rival any cult, and deception had so seeped into their other teachings and practices that it would have to be considered a cult, renouncing or perverting the very basic doctrines of the faith. I felt that this whole perversion began with the leader falling into an affair, but instead of repenting, he tried to justify it. Again, sin is deceitful, and if you practice it, you will be deceived.

I know a number of professional athletes who had to quit going to church because of pastors hitting on their wives. What are those shepherds going to say to the Lord on Judgment Day for having done this to His sheep? How many innocent souls in pursuit of the Lord happen upon this kind of evil behavior in a church or movement and are derailed? Remember, the Lord Jesus Himself said that it would be better for a millstone to be hung around our neck and be cast into the sea than to cause even one of His little ones to stumble (see Matthew 18:6).

When weird practices or doctrines start to manifest in a group, leave as fast as you can. Such groups will almost always try to bind you to them with a control spirit, guilt, and fears that you will miss the will of God for your life, that you are "touching the anointed," or other yokes of bondage. Do not listen to them; do not fear them; and do not let them control you—leave as fast as you can! Do not stay to try to help others. It is very unlikely that you will be able to help anyone by staying, but you will be putting yourself and your family in jeopardy.

Again, these are extreme examples that I have seen with those I do think had extraordinary anointing from the Lord, but when sin entered, it led to an even deeper and extraordinary deception and perversion. I can understand why, after seeing this, that some would determine to not want to be in leadership or grow in their anointing. That is not the answer because then the devil has already won. The answer is to heed the warning of I Corinthians 10:12: **"Therefore let him who thinks he stands take heed lest he fall."**

The Great Deception

If we ever start to think that we are so wise and strong in the Lord that we cannot fall, then a fall is inevitable. Pride caused the devil to fall in the first place, and it has been at the root of almost every fall since. There seems to be a pride with many who are used with a great anointing; sometimes they get to the place where they think they are somehow special and will get away with such things because of the way God has used them. This is a terrible presumption that the Lord Jesus Himself addressed in Matthew 7:21-23:

"Not everyone who says to Me, 'Lord, Lord,' will enter the kingdom of heaven; but he who does the will of My Father who is in heaven.

"Many will say to Me on that day, 'Lord, Lord, did we not prophesy in Your name, and in Your name cast out demons, and in Your name perform many miracles?'

"And then I will declare to them, 'I never knew you; depart from Me, you who practice lawlessness.'"

Lawlessness is the result of rationalizing away the clear Word of God. It is the tendency to bend the rules in order to get away with something. That tendency is also called **"craftiness"** in Scripture (see Ephesians 4:14), and was the very first attribute given to describe the devil in the Garden. Once you start down the path of bending the rules, you have opened the door very wide to Satan, and he will come through it. Even the antichrist is called **"the mystery of lawlessness,"** (see **II Thessalonians 2:7**) and **"the man of lawlessness"** (see **II Thessalonians 2:3**).

I have been told by Christian leaders that when I preach these things, a great fear comes upon them. I hope it does. I hope it has come upon all who read this, for your sakes. We are in great need of the pure and holy fear of the Lord. As we are told in Proverbs 9:10, **"The fear of the Lord is the beginning of wisdom."** We are also told in

Proverbs 8:13, **"The fear of the Lord is to hate evil; pride and arrogance and the evil way."** The fear of the Lord is the beginning of wisdom, and those who stay on the path of life never lose it. However, it is not the highest form of wisdom.

Love is the highest wisdom, but true love is built upon a strong foundation of the fear of the Lord. We should fear the consequences of sin, understanding that God's judgment is going to come upon the world for these things. However, we should hate sin even more because of what it does to the One we love, and what sin did to Him on the cross, which He bore for our redemption. How could anyone who has truly beheld the cross not hate that which caused our King so much pain?

Please read the following Scriptures carefully and read all Scripture quotations. The Scriptures are the Word of God and are far more powerful for changing us than anything I could write. If any of these verses especially speak to you about a stronghold in your life, write them down on 3 x 5 cards and read them as often as you need to in order to combat the temptations in your life. It is the truth of His Word that sets us free!

For the law of the Spirit of life in Christ Jesus has set you free from the law of sin and of death.

For what the Law could not do, weak as it was through the flesh, God did: sending His own Son in the likeness of sinful flesh

and as an offering for sin, He condemned sin in the flesh,

in order that the requirement of the Law might be fulfilled in us, who do not walk according to the flesh, but according to the Spirit.

For those who are according to the flesh set their minds on the things of the flesh, but those who are according to the Spirit, the things of the Spirit.

For the mind set on the flesh is death, but the mind set on the Spirit is life and peace,

because the mind set on the flesh is hostile toward God; for it does not subject itself to the law of God, for it is not even able to do so;

and those who are in the flesh cannot please God.

However, you are not in the flesh but in the Spirit, if indeed the Spirit of God dwells in you. But if anyone does not have the Spirit of Christ, he does not belong to Him.

And if Christ is in you, though the body is dead because of sin, yet the spirit is alive because of righteousness.

But if the Spirit of Him who raised Jesus from the dead dwells in you, He who raised Christ Jesus from the dead will also give life to your mortal bodies through His Spirit who indwells you (Romans 8:2-11).

We will go over more encouraging and edifying principles of how our hearts are purified and changed, but it is necessary for us to understand sin and that it is the path to death. If we want to live, we must turn from sin and look to the One Who alone is Life. He will give us His own Holy Spirit so that we can live free from the yoke of sin, living instead a life of righteousness, holiness, and truth.

CHAPTER THREE

THE SEEDS OF IMMORALITY

In the last chapter, we began our study of the works of the flesh with immorality. In this chapter, we will examine the next two together, which are related and are also the beginning of transgression that leads to immorality: **"impurity"** and **"sensuality."**

Impurity is the lustful gratification of our own flesh through such things as pornography, fantasizing, and masturbation. To follow this path will lead to a basic type of disrespect that we have for ourselves. Because it is not possible to love others the way that we should if we do not love ourselves as we should, impurity and lust are fundamental attacks on our development into who God created us to be. The answer to this is not to just reject impurity, but rather to devote ourselves to purity, walking in the dignity and respect that we should have for ourselves as the true royalty on the earth—the sons and daughters of the King.

Sensuality is the tendency to try to be sexually attractive to someone other than our spouse, causing us, at the very least, to become stumbling blocks by encouraging the lust of others. The answer to this problem is not to refuse to appreciate beauty or to try to become unattractive, such as not wearing makeup or attractive clothes. That will lead to a form of legalism which will have no true effect on combating lust. One can be attractive without being sensual and without exciting lust in others. There is a dignity and honor with which the sons and daughters of the King of kings should behave and carry themselves. "The beauty of holiness" is actually much more attractive than lustful beauty could ever be because it draws out of people both dignity and respect. The Apostle Paul stated it powerfully in I Thessalonians 4:3-8:

> **For this is the will of God, your sanctification; that is, that you abstain from sexual immorality;**
>
> **that each of you know how to possess his own vessel in sanctification and honor,**
>
> **not in lustful passion, like the Gentiles who do not know God;**
>
> **and that no man transgress and defraud his brother in the matter because the Lord is the avenger in all these things, just as we also told you before and solemnly warned you.**
>
> **For God has not called us for the purpose of impurity, but in sanctification.**

Consequently, he who rejects this is not rejecting man but the God who gives His Holy Spirit to you.

There are some foolish souls who believe that because they have never committed an actual act of immorality that they are living a holy life, when in fact they are addicted to pornography or practicing other impure or sensual behavior. This is a deception which can also lead to the hardness of heart and the kinds of deception that we discussed in the last chapter.

A Healthy Life

The primary way to keep from falling to perversion is to have a healthy sex life. Sex was created by God as a special gift to His creation, a wonderful way for a man and woman to bond and express their love for each other when in a committed marriage relationship. Having a great sex life is spiritual warfare against the lust that permeates the world. It takes a positive to cast out the negative. The vision for a good sex life should be taught in church. If a vision for sex as it was intended, with the dignity and honor that it deserves was imparted, then the perversion of it would not have such inroads into Christians' lives.

Sex in the marriage relationship edifies, and it is a foundation for a healthy marriage. Note that I did not say that it is *the* foundation, but it is an important one. Sex outside of marriage destroys. It is that simple. Sex outside of marriage may briefly gratify one physically, but there will be inevitable emotional and spiritual damage done every time. You may not think that it does, but the thief is using it to pervert your soul and move you further from the most fulfilling relationship that you could have on the earth, which God has planned for you.

Likewise, impurity and sensuality damage our souls by setting us on a course of being led by lust rather than love. Lust and love are in opposition to each other. Lust is motivated by self-centeredness, and love is motivated by care for others. To the degree that lust is able to grip our lives, we will be in opposition to the Spirit of God, who is Love. Impurity and sensuality are the primary ways that lust gains an entrance into our lives and are primary obstacles that will be used to keep us from growing up into Christ. As we are told in Romans 6:19:

> **For just as you presented your members as slaves to impurity and to lawlessness, resulting in further lawlessness, so now present your members as slaves to righteousness, resulting in sanctification.**

As this verse illuminates, impurity is one of the primary open doors to lawlessness, which will be one of the greatest evils to come upon the world at the end of this age. If we start compromising with our own bodies, which are temples of the Holy Spirit, then we will soon start compromising the clear truth of the Word of God. We will then be led more by self-will than by the Spirit. As the Apostle Paul also wrote in Romans 6:1-11:

> What shall we say then? Are we to continue in sin that grace might increase?

> May it never be! How shall we who died to sin still live in it?

> Or do you not know that all of us who have been baptized into Christ Jesus have been baptized into His death?

> Therefore we have been buried with Him through baptism into death, in order that as Christ was raised from the dead through the glory of the Father, so we too might walk in newness of life.

> For if we have become united with Him in the likeness of His death, certainly we shall be also in the likeness of His resurrection,

> knowing this, that our old self was crucified with Him, that our body of sin might be done away with, that we should no longer be slaves to sin;

> for he who has died is freed from sin.

> Now if we have died with Christ, we believe that we shall also live with Him,

knowing that Christ, having been raised from the dead, is never to die again; death no longer is master over Him.

For the death that He died, He died to sin, once for all; but the life that He lives, He lives to God.

Even so consider yourselves to be dead to sin, but alive to God in Christ Jesus.

Being free from the sins of impurity and sensuality are the result of our loving God and loving those whom He has joined us to more than the desires of our flesh. If we will take those desires to the cross, they will be resurrected in something far more fulfilling than anything trying to fulfill our lusts could ever produce—a relationship where we can become one in body, soul, and spirit.

The Lord wants to give us life and give it far more abundantly than we can even imagine. That is why recent studies have shown consistently that Christians tend to have better sex lives than non-Christians. The Christians who do not have fulfilling sex lives are almost always the ones who have slipped into some form of seeking sexual gratification in an illegal way.

Lust can never satisfy us, but rather will keep us always seeking satisfaction without any possibility of ever really getting it. Love alone can lead to our true satisfaction. Love is what the Lord wants for us—that it would be the guiding motivation of our lives. This is first a love for Him by which we would never want to do anything that is displeasing to Him, and then such a love for others that we would never want to use anyone selfishly in any way.

With the overwhelming onslaught of sensuality in the West, it will take a supreme devotion to keep ourselves pure in this environment. This may be one reason why the Lord gave His greatest promises to the overcomers of the church at Laodicea, the last church that He addressed, which in many ways was a prophecy to the last-day church. Our love for the Lord and our love for others will have to grow correspondingly if we are going to assault lust, impurity, and sensuality in our time. It will be possibly the greatest battle, but perhaps it is also the greatest opportunity.

In all things remember this—love is the answer. This is not just a cliché. The answer to overcoming evil is being filled with the Spirit and growing in the fruit of the Spirit. We must resolve to never rationalize the clear Word of God; we must call sin what it is—sin. It is not justifiable under any circumstance. It will lead to death in all circumstances. Life is found by loving God and loving one another.

CHAPTER FOUR
IDOLATRY

We continue in this chapter with the next in the list of the works of the flesh—**"idolatry."** We may think that no one worships idols anymore, but in fact it is widespread in every nation and culture, including all of the nations of the West, and even among Christians. How could any Christian ever fall to worshiping idols? This is one of the most important questions we can ask. It is one of the most subtle and devastating sins of the heart which befalls many Christians.

An idol is not just an inanimate object that one bows down to and worships—it is anything that we put our trust in or give our affections to more than God. This can include money, our jobs, our education, our country, our spouse, our children, sports, our pastor, favorite teacher or author, or just about anything. It is no accident that famous athletes and entertainers are often called "idols," as many people's affection and devotion to them can easily eclipse their affection and devotion to God.

Idolatry comes in many forms. The most common idols in the West are wealth or material possessions, which the Book of Revelation explains will be the ultimate idols in the last days. That is why the mark of the beast is an economic mark, determining if we can buy, sell, or trade. It is imperative for Christians to have sound teaching and a strong foundation in how they handle their money and possessions.

Good Is the Enemy of Best

One of the most deceptive and devastating forms of idolatry that has gained a widespread following in the church is the worship of the things of God in place of God. There are many Christians, especially Christian leaders, who worship the church or ministry more than God. There are many who worship the Bible, prayer, and the gifts of the Spirit more than they worship God.

It is common for those who are in "the ministry" to let the ministry become the focus of their devotion over their personal relationship with the Lord. It was because I saw this happening in myself that I once left the ministry for seven years. I felt that my personal relationship with God had become increasingly shallow, and I felt that I had to get back to Him or I would ultimately be a failure in my calling. When we exalt the church or ministry above the Lord, we may claim to be leading people to the Lord, but they are in fact being led to us.

Ministry for God becomes an idol when it becomes our main devotion instead of the means to God that it is meant to be. To counter this, I have heard some preachers say that we should seek the Giver and not the gifts. That may sound wise, but is in fact contradictory to the Scripture, which tells us to seek the gifts. Such an overreaction can actually lead to even worse transgressions. As the Lord Jesus Himself made clear to us, if we do not seek to know and use the gifts that He has given to us, we are guilty of burying the talents that He has entrusted to us, and are the ones He called "wicked, lazy slaves!" (see Matthew 25:26)

In dealing with the works of the flesh, we need to beware of mere human remedies that often seem wise, but in fact lead to other, sometimes even worse problems. Again, there is a ditch on either side of the path of life. Those who are prone to overreact to extremes will inevitably fall to the opposite extreme. It is wisdom to seek the Giver more than the gifts, but it is wisdom and obedience to His Word to seek the gifts as well. Those who understand spiritual gifts come to understand that seeking the gifts is, in fact, one way that we seek God Himself. The gifts of the Spirit are God Himself working through us.

True Love

The wise seek everything they can get from God, but they seek God Himself even more. Those who foolishly think that they should not seek anything from God, but just trust Him to give them what He wants them to have, have a flawed understanding of God and His ways. He only gives to those who care for His gifts enough to ask.

Some do not want to seek the gifts or other benefits from God until they feel like they deserve it. That is the root of a religious spirit, not the Spirit of God. We can never earn anything that we get from God. Those who think they must wait to deserve what they get will never receive anything from Him, including their salvation. Those who hold to such unbiblical teachings or practices inevitably become bound and deceived by a religious spirit that they serve in place of God. This is another form of idolatry because we worship our own performance rather than God.

We should settle it now that we will never be wise enough, mature enough, or righteous enough to deserve anything from God, but that we are going to pursue everything He will give to us! We do not want to be like the elder brother in the Parable of the Prodigal Son who had access to all that his father had, but did not use it, and because of this became jealous of his brother. Jealousy is one of the most deadly sins, and we are told that envy was the reason why Jesus was crucified. We must come to the Lord being as foolish and unrighteous as the prodigal son because we all are. We do not deserve to even be a slave in His house, but we are foolish to turn down a single thing God wants to give us, including the full inheritance as a son.

However, we do not want to come to Him presumptuously either. Some think that they can claim or demand their inheritance, which Scripture also clearly shows is a tragic mistake. Again, there is a ditch on either side of the path of life. We should come to

Him as sons and daughters, but also with humility, having the utmost respect for our Father, and knowing how undeserving we are, just as the prodigal did. We should also come asking Him to give us the wisdom to handle His gifts and resources rightly, realizing that we are not wise or righteous enough for any of this without Him.

We also must pursue Him more than anything that He can give us. Erskine Holt, who recently passed away after more than half a century of traveling and ministering, once told me a story that I will never forget. He had just returned home from an extensive trip, and had spent almost a whole day seeking a perfect gift for his wife. When he walked in to see her, he gave it to her and could not wait for her to open it. She looked at the package and threw it in the trash saying, "I don't want a gift—I want you!"

Of course, that meant more to him than her joy in any gift could have. I asked him the same question you may be thinking, and yes, she did later dig the gift out of the trash. Gifts are good too, but must never become greater than our love for God or His people.

Anything that we have affection for or trust in can begin to eclipse God in our affections and trust. However, the way to avoid idolatry is not to love these less, but to love God more. It is also wrong to not put some trust in other people, but we must always trust in God more. If we love God more than we love others, we will love them more than we would otherwise. If we trust God more than we trust anyone or anything else, we are free to trust others far more than we would otherwise.

The things we love and have put our trust in are usually gifts from God that He wants us to appreciate and love. As we are told in Psalm 37:4-5: **"Delight yourself in the Lord; and He will give you the desires of your heart. Commit your way to the Lord, trust also in Him, and He will do it."** The Lord loves to give good gifts to His children. He loves to see their delight in the gifts. He just does not want the gifts to eclipse our love for Him and delight in Him.

Mike Bickle has been one of my favorite preachers and people since I first met him back in 1988. I think few people have a passion for the Lord like Mike does. He lives for prayer and may have logged more time in prayer rooms than anyone else alive today. However, when he started the prayer movement called the International House of Prayer (IHOP), he had the wisdom to call it "the harp and bowl" ministry, combining worship and intercession. All prayer that is just intercession without the affection of worship can become a dead form and can itself become an idol. It is a good thing to see this model of combined prayer and worship sweeping across the worldwide body of Christ.

Now the point of these teachings is not just so we learn some things, but so we will be changed by them, becoming vessels fit for the Master's use. We are examining these works of the flesh so that we can repent of any that may have a grip on our lives. The answer to sexual lust is not to give up sex, but to develop a healthy sex life with your spouse, or if you do not have a spouse, as the Scripture implores, get one!

The answer to idolatry is not to give up having affection for anyone or anything else, but to love God more. He is more interesting, wonderful, attractive, compelling, and desirable than anything or anyone else. Let us not keep depriving ourselves by not taking full advantage of the relationship that we can have with Him. Your day, or your life, will only be successful to the degree that you have walked with Him in it. We will measure the success of our lives by how we have loved God in them.

WITCHCRAFT

The next work of the flesh that is listed in this text in Galatians is **"sorcery"** or witchcraft. Certainly no true Christian would ever become involved in witchcraft, but the truth is that most are, even if unknowingly. How can this be?

First, we often think of witchcraft in its extreme forms of black magic and devil worshipers. But, like many of the works of evil, there is often a subtle, seemingly harmless or even benevolent form of them that entraps those who really do not mean to bring harm to anyone. They may even have good intentions, but are using a form of witchcraft nonetheless.

Witchcraft is counterfeit spiritual authority and is used to manipulate and control others. It is using any spirit other than the Holy Spirit. This can be done to accomplish our own purpose, even a noble purpose or something we feel called to do for the Lord. We may wonder how someone would try to use witchcraft or soul power to accomplish the works of God, but many have tried, causing some of the worst spiritual disasters in church history right up to the present. A noble purpose does not justify evil means. Tacking the Lord's name onto a project does not mean that the Lord is behind it.

The Dignity of Royalty

The Lord, being the King of kings, above all rule, authority, power, and dominion, moves with a certain dignity in all that He does and is far above such things as trying to manipulate others or using a dominating form of control—so do those who move by His Spirit in true spiritual authority.

As stated, it is not only possible, but common for people to try to accomplish the purposes of God using what is in fact counterfeit spiritual authority or witchcraft. They manipulate people into giving to their cause or use a form of control to keep them committed and to get the job done. These are houses that we may claim are being built for the Lord, but He will not bless them with His manifest presence. This is like King David trying to bring the ark of God to Jerusalem on a new ox cart. Oxen speak of natural strength in Scripture, and we often think we can bring God to our place in our own strength. David paid the price for this foolishness, and so do many well-meaning, but misled Christians.

My daughter and I recently stopped in several used car lots to find her something to drive to college. Two of them were a joy to visit and the salespeople delightful. They wanted to sell us a car, but we did not feel any pressure at all. The third car dealer we visited was the opposite. I do not remember ever being subjected to such base manipulation in any potential business transaction. As we left, my daughter said she felt "slimed." The whole experience was similar to what I think it would be like to get your hand caught in a meat grinder. I resolved to never step foot on that car lot again and would certainly never buy a car from them. You could feel hype and manipulation throughout that business. Sadly, it reminded me of some churches I have been in. The salesmen felt like some preachers I have met.

The Carnal Respond to Carnal Authority

Most churches are more like the first two car dealers we visited, conducting their business with dignity and respect for their people, without hype or manipulation. However, the reason that the third car dealer can stay in business, and the reason churches that are like it stay open, is because of the great number of people who allow themselves to be so manipulated and controlled. As Paul the Apostle lamented in II Corinthians 11:20:

> **For you bear with anyone if he enslaves you, if he devours you, if he takes advantage of you, if he exalts himself, if he hits you in the face.**

One reason why the Corinthians could also have had such base forms of carnality manifested in their church was probably the result of the kind of authority they responded to, which Paul addressed in the verse above. Carnal people respond to carnal authority. Such overbearing authority will not cast out the carnal nature, but feed it. Only the Spirit can beget that which is Spirit.

We can continue to reproach the Corinthian church in our hearts and teachings, but it is likely that if they existed today, they would be the most spiritual church on the planet in spite of their many flaws. Because most people, including most Christians as recent studies have proven, do, in fact, live in a place of basic carnality, car dealers and churches like the ones I briefly described above not only continue in business, but actually thrive. However, one thing we can count on is that many temporary successes will prove to be ultimate failures, as we are told in I Corinthians 3:10-13:

> **According to the grace of God which was given to me, as a wise master builder I laid a foundation, and another is building upon it. But let each man be careful how he builds upon it.**

> **For no man can lay a foundation other than the one which is laid, which is Jesus Christ.**

> **Now if any man builds upon the foundation with gold, silver, precious stones, wood, hay, straw,**

> **each man's work will become evident; for the day will show it, because it is to be**

revealed with fire; and the fire itself will test the quality of each man's work.

Works or accomplishments which are the fruit of the works of the flesh, or carnal strength, will have to be maintained by the flesh. The bigger such works become, the more striving will be required to maintain them and so the manipulation and control grows, until the leaders and the people break under the pressure. This is where you find throughout history the long train of devastated works and people who were supposed to be doing the work of the Lord.

In politics, business, and sometimes even in family relations, these forms of manipulation and control can seem to be almost the fabric upon which all human relations are built. This is true to a large degree in this age. It will not be true of the kingdom or those works that really are being built by the King.

Drugs and Witchcraft

Now I have dealt with this form of witchcraft superficially, as we have in fact dealt with the other works of the flesh superficially as well. We can only go so deep in a format such as this; however, I do want to touch on one more increasingly popular form of witchcraft—the use of drugs.

The words "sorcery" and "witchcraft" both mean to call on or conjure other spirits, which God's people have always been strictly forbidden to do. We cannot serve the Lord and demons. It is noteworthy that the Greek word translated **"sorcery"** and **"witchcraft"** in the New Testament is *pharmakeia,* from which we derive our English word "pharmacy."

There is a reason why a large part of black magic involves making concoctions that supposedly empower those who take them with supernatural powers. It works. Does this mean that taking drugs can open us up to demons? We need to distinguish between those drugs that are meant to provide healing to our bodies and those that are for the purpose of altering our consciousness. If we are purposely taking mind-altering drugs, we can open ourselves to demonic oppression. Continued practice can lead to increasing oppression, which leads to demonic possession to the degree that we no longer have control over ourselves, but the devil does.

There is a relationship between the increasing debauchery of our time and the increasing use of illegal drugs. This is a gate of hell which the devil is pouring through. Do not open this gate to him in your own life. Let us also resolve that we do not want one thing in our lives that God does not want us to have. Therefore, we will pursue what we are to have and the works that we are to do by His Spirit, which is always recognized by the fruit of the Spirit.

CHAPTER SIX
ENMITIES

In this chapter, we will continue our study of the works of the flesh with **"enmities."** The Greek word that is translated here is *thumos,* which is sometimes translated "fierceness," "indignation," "wrath," "hostility," or "hatred." Of course all of these are very prevalent in the world, but none of them are acceptable for Christians. In my search of the Scriptures, I have only found two things that are legal for us to hate—sin and unrighteousness. To hate anything or anyone else actually opens the door for evil to prevail, not righteousness.

The Devil Hates

Does this mean that we should not hate the devil? Does God hate the devil? Would He tell us to love our enemies and then hate His? The Lord hates the devil's works, and He hates man's evil works, sin, and unrighteousness, but He does not hate the devil, and He does not hate even the most evil men. In fact, the Scriptures are clear that He loves all men and desires for them to be saved. Will they be cast into the lake of fire? Yes. But they will not be cast into it out of hatred, but because He has to do that which will forever purge evil and unrighteousness from His creation.

My point is that we must also rise above taking offenses against us personally, which is the usual inroad of strife and enmities. As we are told in Ephesians 6:12, **"For our struggle is not against flesh and blood, but against the rulers, against the powers, against the world forces of this darkness, against the spiritual forces of wickedness in the heavenly places."** When people wrong us, or do evil things, we must rise above taking it as a personal offense from that person, and know that there is something much bigger behind it. Anger or hatred will blind us to the truth, or what is truly happening. If we are going to see anything accurately, we must see through the eyes of the Spirit, and that means we will be seeing through the fruit of the Spirit.

Now we may think that our victory is to cast down those principalities and any evil thing that is causing people to do evil to one another. That is true ultimately, but the immediate victory may have more to do with us personally. The Lord is not doing this evil thing to us, but He is allowing it. The reason why He allows any bad thing to happen to His people is for the sake of conforming us to the image of His Son. Our victory in the situation will come when we love that person, or people, in spite of any wrong done to us. This is not permitting evil, but as we are instructed in Romans 12:21: **"Do not be overcome by evil, but overcome evil with good."**

Casting Out Demons

Satan will not cast out Satan. That means that hatred or retaliation will not resolve other wrongs, but actually multiplies the evil in the situation, giving the devil even more power over it. As the Lord Himself explained in Matthew 12:28: **"But if I cast out demons by the Spirit of God, then the kingdom of God has come upon you."** There is no room in a Christian for enmity or hatred of another person, regardless of what they have done.

Does this mean that we should have compassion on the devil? No. Neither does it mean that we should have compassion on those who are doing evil, but it may. There is a difference between love and compassion, though true compassion is always rooted in love. I do not want to over-complicate this issue; there are options for how we respond to wrongs committed against us, but one of those options is never to let hatred or enmity get a place in our lives.

There are times when we must turn the other cheek to evil, and there are times when it is biblically right to seek to recover damages from those who have wrongly attacked us. However, when this is the right path, we must still do it in the right spirit, not out of retaliation. We may need to seek compensation for the sake of such things as being a good steward of what has been entrusted to us or even to help wake up the person who is doing evil, but not just to get even with them.

Does this mean that Christians should be free to sue those who have wronged them? Yes. There are times when it is right to do this. That is essentially what Paul the Apostle did when he appealed to Caesar; he was suing the nation of Israel for wrongly accusing and attacking him. However, he was not doing this to retaliate against Israel. As he wrote to the Romans before arriving there for his trial, he said that he loved the Jews so much he would even give up his own salvation if it would result in them being saved. He was actually suing them because he loved them and wanted the truth to come out about what they were doing, or he simply did not feel that in this situation he should give in to the injustice.

Again, there is a ditch on either side of the path of life. We are not to hate anyone, because we do not want hatred to get a grip on us, but that does not mean we cannot defend ourselves when wronged. We just have to do it in the right spirit when we do it. Paul and the other apostles often defended themselves against others who wrongly accused them. However, it does seem that they were only doing this for the sake of those who were being deceived by the accusers, not out of self-preservation. There is a difference.

We need to also recognize the times that the Lord does not want us to defend ourselves, but turn the other cheek. Sometimes this is because He wants to defend us, which is always much better than trying to defend ourselves.

Sometimes, the Lord may not want us to defend ourselves. He wants the situation to work a deeper character change in us, or He may want to deal with our pride. In these cases, He may have us turn the other cheek, and then He may not defend us either. This may seem like allowing evil and injustice to prevail, but He has higher purposes. Regardless of whether the Lord chooses to defend us or not, in every case He wants us to abide in His Spirit, which means love, peace, patience, and other fruit.

The Devil's Poison

Those, including Christians, who give themselves to bitterness or resentment will end up doing much evil. We must learn to recognize that every chance we have to become resentful is also a chance to grow in the nature of Christ, who did not become resentful of even the ones who nailed Him to the cross, but actually suffered all that He did for their sakes. If we are going to become like Him, which is the basic calling of every Christian, we must learn to take up our crosses every day, resolving to also lay down our own lives, our own rights, and maybe our own reputations, for the sake of even those who are attacking us.

I was recently asked "to discern" some statements made by a man who was upset by a conference in Kansas City that some friends of mine had hosted, and had therefore "left the prophetic movement" (whatever that means). The statements that I was shown were so full of enmity that I was shocked any Christian could not discern the source of them. The truth is not many Christians have discernment in such things. However, there is one biblical measure of discernment that is very clear, James 3:13-18:

> **Who among you is wise and understanding? Let him show by his good behavior his deeds in the gentleness of wisdom.**

> **But if you have bitter jealousy and selfish ambition in your heart, do not be arrogant and so lie against the truth.**

> **This wisdom is not that which comes down from above, but is earthly, natural, demonic.**

> **For where jealousy and selfish ambition exist, there is disorder and every evil thing.**

> **But the wisdom from above is first pure, then peaceable, gentle, reasonable, full of mercy and good fruits, unwavering, without hypocrisy.**

> **And the seed whose fruit is righteousness is sown in peace by those who make peace.**

Soon it came to light that the man who wrote with such enmity against the conference in Kansas City, its hosts, and then the whole prophetic movement, had sought to be recognized and given a platform at the conference in order to steer it in the direction he thought it should go. He was so pushy and full of the wrong spirit that they refused to give him any platform and would not allow him access to the hospitality room to get at the other speakers. He was offended by this. Almost everyone who had an encounter with this man said that he had a foul spirit. It sure sounds like selfish ambition, jealousy, and what is clearly stated in James 3, which is not the wisdom that comes down from above, but from below. Yet, he has an extensive Internet following, and many seem to even appreciate his poison.

At this time, there really is not much true discernment in the body of Christ, and those who are in direct violation of the James 3 standard of having "wisdom from above" can still affect many people. If this man has, in fact, removed himself from any association with the prophetic, I think we should be thankful. I was actually impressed that those who led that prophetic conference discerned the spirit which this man was operating in and removed him. We cannot allow people like that to hijack our conferences, our churches, or our movements. When they prevail, as with the abortion movement, the endeavor will end up in defeat.

I concur that abortion is one of the greatest evils of our time and probably reflects the greatest depths of depravity that the human soul can fall to. Even the beasts will sacrifice their own lives to protect their young, and for us to slay ours when they are in the most helpless state is possibly the greatest reflection of how low mankind has actually fallen. However, when I see Christians raging with obvious hatred against young women who are going to have an abortion, or those who perform them, I know that we are going to lose that battle. If we are going to cast out that spirit, we must do it as the Lord said—by the Spirit of God. Hatred and rage are not listed as fruit of the Spirit and will never be a part of what He does.

The church in America could have already won the war against abortion if so many of the leaders of the anti-abortion movement had not been so full of enmity, and they had rather resolved not to return evil for evil, but to overcome evil with good in the right Spirit. The same is true in the battle against homosexuality. The homosexuals who are demanding total tolerance from everyone else seem to be by far the most intolerant of any group. I have never witnessed more rage and cruelty than can come out of homosexual activists when they are confronted, except maybe what comes out of Christians who start giving into enmity and responding in the same spirit. The evil is multiplied in both, and the consequences will not favor the kingdom of God in that case.

We will never be able to cast out that spirit by our rage and intolerance. This does not mean that we compromise with what the Bible clearly states is a sin, a perversion, and an abomination. I do not intend to ever compromise my position on this issue, and I have and will continue to apologize to homosexuals for the way some Christians have treated them. I intend to treat homosexuals with dignity and respect, as I will every other human being that was made in the image of God. I do not intend to compromise my convictions about the sin and the desperate need of the sinner for the salvation of the cross, but I have also resolved to love even those who are gripped in the worst perversion.

As we are told in James 1:19-20, **"But let everyone be quick to hear, slow to speak and slow to anger; for the anger of man does not achieve the righteousness of God."** Do not let enmity have any place in your life. When it tries to get a grip on you today, which it surely will since the Lord honors us with opportunities to take up our crosses, resolve to **"overcome evil with good" (see Romans 12:21).**

CHAPTER SEVEN

STRIFE

The next work of the flesh in this study is **"strife."** This is from the Greek word, *eritheia,* which is usually translated "contention" but also could be translated "intrigue." By implication, this is the tendency to secretly spread discord or enmity. This is an evil that can be found in almost every congregation, every organization, and in many families. It has probably done more damage to the church than all of the cults and persecutions combined.

Reaping and Sowing

These intrigues that lead to division between believers often come with the pretense of having the people's or the Lord's interests at heart. However, this is at best a work of the flesh and often is used to open a wide gate of hell into the church, as well as into the lives of those who use such devices. As we are promised in Galatians 6:7, **"Do not be deceived, God is not mocked; for whatever a man sows, this he will also reap."** Those who trouble others inevitably lead very troubled lives themselves.

As intrigue implies doing things secretly, anything that cannot be done in the light of openness is darkness and is going to be evil. The devil dwells in darkness, and that which has to be kept in darkness is usually from him. It is for this reason that we should be wary of anyone who wants to tell us a secret about someone else. I have never seen good or edification come from this. In times of persecution, there may be things that obviously have to be done secretly, but other than that, the things that are done in secret are rarely going to be righteous unless they are our secret prayers and gifts.

As we have discussed before, let us never forget the prayer that the Lord made on His last night before His crucifixion, which is recorded in John 17. He knew that He only had a short time left on this earth to pray as a man. If we knew that we only had a few hours left in this life, our prayers would certainly be focused on the things that are the most important to us. We can therefore believe that this prayer is possibly the greatest reflection of the things that were on our Lord's heart. The main theme of that prayer is the unity of His people. If unity is so important to Him, then those who truly love Him would never do anything intentionally to bring strife or division to His people.

I know that as a parent there are few things that grieve me more than strife among my children. There are few things that give me more pleasure than seeing them getting along with each other and enjoying one another. Our Father in heaven is the same way. It brings great pleasure to Him to see His children loving each other. It brings great grief to Him for us to fight with each other. Using intrigue to bring division is especially sinister. Such has the hallmarks of the nature of the devil himself, about whom it was said in the beginning that he was **"crafty" (see Genesis 3:1)**.

When Hell Agrees

When we become offended or bothered by something going on in the church, or with other people, we often seek the comfort of having other people agree with us. However, that is an agreement from hell. This is how the devil, whose title is "the accuser of the brethren," (see Revelation 12:10) usually gains entry and begins to do his most evil deeds, which are to separate God's people from one another. The devil seems to understand even better than most Christians that the unity of God's people multiplies their power. Therefore, his primary strategy against the church is to keep God's people divided. We must wake up to this strategy and not allow ourselves to be used in anything that brings division among God's people.

One way that the devil often tries to get Christians to justify their evil intrigue is by having them use prayer as a motive. Some of the worst strife in the body begins with someone sharing someone else's problems or perceived problems in order "to pray for them." Some of the most diabolical gossip is uttered in prayers. Some even use prayer as a form of witchcraft in order to try to dictate policy in their church. This has not only defiled many people, but it is often used to destroy the very prayer ministry in a church. Regardless of whether you call it prayer or not, this form of trying to manipulate and control others is a form of witchcraft.

Anointed Curses

There is also an evil that some call "anointed curses." These are released when Christians use something holy, such as prayer, to speak evil of others or over others. Words do have power, as we are told in Proverbs 18:21, **"Death and life are in the power of the tongue...."** Are our words giving life or death?

You will never see the King of kings or His true servants stoop to using intrigue to do His work. All such devices are from the devil. We need to recognize them, refuse to participate in them, and as need be rebuke those who do. True shepherds and true watchmen will rise up and confront evil that tries to attack God's people, and this is one of the devil's most deadly schemes.

We need to also challenge those who fall to such devices for their sake. As the Lord Himself warned, it would be better not to be born than to become a stumbling block to even the least of His little ones. After issuing this warning, the Lord then gave us a procedure that would help keep us from becoming stumbling blocks. He said if a brother was in sin, we were to first go to him in private. If we have not been to the person with what we think is wrong with him, and then go to any other person with it, is a transgression that can place us in jeopardy of being a stumbling block, which is probably far worse than the sin he is committing.

Spiritual Ones Restore

After we have been through the first step outlined by the Lord in Matthew 18 for addressing sin in someone's life, if they do not receive it and come to repentance, only then should we ever take the issue to another person, and only in order to help the person who is sinning with their problem. If this has failed, which often means giving the person time to see his sin and repent (the Lord even gave Jezebel time to repent), only then should it be brought before the church. However, even that is done for the purpose of bringing the repentance that leads to restoration. As we are also told in Galatians 6:1:

> **Brethren, even if a man is caught in any trespass, you who are spiritual, restore such a one in a spirit of gentleness; each one looking to yourself, lest you too be tempted.**

Here we see that the truly spiritual people restore. If our motives for saying something negative about another person are anything other than restoration, then they are almost certainly evil. If anyone approaches us with something they say has to be kept a secret, then refuse to hear it. It will only lead to evil.

If it cannot be kept in the light, then it is darkness. As we are told in Ephesians 4:29-32:

> **Let no unwholesome word proceed from your mouth, but only such a word as is good for edification according to the need of the moment, that it may give grace to those who hear.**
>
> **And do not grieve the Holy Spirit of God, by whom you were sealed for the day of redemption.**
>
> **Let all bitterness and wrath and anger and clamor and slander be put away from you, along with all malice.**
>
> **And be kind to one another, tender-hearted, forgiving each other, just as God in Christ also has forgiven you.**

Here we are told how not to grieve the Holy Spirit by putting away all **"bitterness and wrath and anger and clamor and slander . . . along with all malice."** Nothing so offends the Holy Spirit as these things. In their place we are to instead be kind, forgiving, and tender-hearted toward each other. We can know those who are true Christians by their love for one another. We can also recognize those who have been sent to do the devil's bidding by the way that they spread strife in the body.

If we are abiding in Christ, then our words will be what He would say in a situation. We do need to ask the question: "WWJD: What would Jesus do?" And "WWJS: What would Jesus say?" Think about this exhortation, **"Let no unwholesome word proceed from your mouth, but only such a word as is good for edification according to the need of the moment, that it may give grace to those who hear."** Do our words impart grace and build up others? Are they the seeds of the fruit of the Spirit, or are they seeds of division, strife, doubt, or fear? As the Lord Jesus Himself stated in Matthew 12:37, **"For by your words you shall be justified, and by your words you shall be condemned."**

Let us be very careful with our words. Because Jesus is the Word, we should have the utmost care for words, seeking to speak those which are from Him. Our words are seeds. What is the fruit of those that we are planting?

CHAPTER EIGHT

JEALOUSY

The next work of the flesh in this study is **"jealousy."** This is another deadly, devastating evil that continues to cause much destruction in the church and in the world. As the Scripture also testifies, it is cruel and unrelenting, destroying the one who has it like it does its victims. The first murder was the result of jealousy, when Cain slew his brother Abel. This was a foreshadowing of how Jesus was to be killed by His brothers, and we are also told that He was crucified because of envy (see Matthew 27:18).

Jealousy obviously should have no place in a Christian. We must learn to recognize even the seeds of jealousy and combat them by using them as an opportunity to grow in the opposite spirit—love that does not seek its own.

Turn Jealousy Into Blessing

Robin McMillan, who is now the pastor of our congregation at Heritage, told me that years ago he had some jealousy rise in his heart when he saw me driving a new car and he was driving an old beat-up one. However, he recognized it for what it was and resolved that instead of being envious, he was going to thank the Lord for blessing me. Then, just a few weeks later he was provided with a new car identical to the one I was driving.

At that same time Robin was the pastor of a small, struggling, but great little congregation. When we felt called to start a congregation not only in the same city, but in the same part of the city, Robin did not become jealous or threatened, but came over and helped us. He encouraged his people to attend our special meetings, and when some of the people in his congregation felt that they were supposed to be a part of our work, he blessed them.

It is one thing for large, successful congregations to do this, but the church Robin was the pastor of was small and struggling. They could not even afford to pay Robin enough to take care of the basic needs of his family. However, the Lord always provided for his needs. Though Robin could not have known it at the time, when he helped us start our church in Charlotte, he was actually providing for his own future, since Robin later became the pastor of our congregation in Charlotte. That could have never happened if he had reacted in a wrong spirit about our starting a church in the same part of town as his.

The True Root of Division

Jealousy among pastors and church leaders is probably the number one reason for most of the division in the body of Christ and is probably the main reason why the Lord can find so few that He can trust with significant spiritual authority. If we are motivated by a work of the flesh, such as jealousy, it will also tempt us to use counterfeit spiritual authority, or witchcraft, for the work. When we are motivated by a work of the flesh, and then try to use another work of the flesh to accomplish the work, we cannot expect the fruit to be good.

One thing I try to watch for the most in people is the sign of jealousy, because I know it will lead to some of the worst problems if given a place. There have been a few times that I put someone in a place of authority, even though there was obvious jealousy working in their lives. I usually did this because they had other gifts or abilities that we needed, but we always paid a high price for this and determined that it was never worth it. It was even more devastating to the people who had it working in their lives, just as we see with Judas and with those who crucified the Lord because of envy. You can even trace some of the world's most devastating problems today to the envy that arose between Ishmael and Isaac.

I likewise marveled at the way other pastors and church leaders in the Charlotte area responded to us while we were establishing our church there. When I felt called to start a church in Charlotte, I dreaded it for a number of reasons. One was that I loved the church that I was a part of at the time and felt a special friendship with its pastor, Randall Worley. I dreaded telling him about the call that I had received, thinking that it could jeopardize our friendship. When I did tell him, I received one of the most wonderful surprises from another Christian leader. His immediate reaction was not one of being threatened, his eyes lit up and he said, "We can send you fifty or sixty of our best people to help you get started!" He was genuinely excited about helping another church get going even though we would be almost next door to him. I almost cried.

To this day, I consider Randall a true friend who can be trusted. He followed through on his word to help us in every way that he could. I did not want him to send us any of his good people, and I really did not want to take people from any other church. However, when some of his folks decided to come over, he always blessed them. When we needed a larger place to hold meetings, he offered his own facilities, which we used many times. His church was actually the birthplace of MorningStar conferences.

Of course, there are some church leaders in Charlotte who not only do not like us, but have publicly accused us of many things which are not true. Some of these have made it a main mission in their lives to attack us, seeming to especially try to fill the Internet with their accusations. Sadly, there is not much true discernment in the church, and many people will believe almost anything posted on the Internet, just as they do things in the media. However, I have been encouraged by the number of people who have read these things and then decided to check us out for themselves. This has led many to us who are now some of our best friends. The negative things written and spoken about us often work as free advertising. They also work to keep the fearful away from us, who will never do well in our kind of ministry.

All things will work together for good if we just love God and follow our calling. The envy that crucified the Lord also led to His greatest promotion of all. We have found that when persecution rises up against us, and it is obviously motivated by jealousy, then we are close to experiencing another major spiritual advance. We need to endure the cross without retaliation, and if we pass the test we are inevitably carried to a higher level. If we become reactionary, it is amazing the way jealousy will begin to manifest in our own hearts. For this reason we try to find any good thing that we can say about those who attack us. We will never overcome evil with retaliation, and we are commanded to overcome evil with good.

The Jealousy Test

There are major tests that will come to us all to help us discern and remove the jealousy from our hearts. We have seen these tests also come upon seemingly the whole body of Christ at times. One of these happened in the late 1980s, in regard to the Kansas City Fellowship (KCF), which was experiencing a remarkable visitation from God at the time. People started coming from all over the world to Kansas City as word spread about what was happening there, especially about the remarkable prophetic ministry taking place. It was a tremendous breath of fresh air to the body of Christ at the time. Then a fellow pastor in Kansas City preached a message accusing KCF of many horrendous things. He circulated the tape more aggressively than anything I have ever witnessed.

When I first heard the tape, I was shocked because I personally knew of some of the incidents he described on the tape, and he was misconstruing them badly, to be generous. I felt there was nothing on the tape that was actually true, but what got my attention was the way the pastor kept comparing his church to KCF in a way that was dripping with jealousy. I did not think anyone could hear this tape and not see that the spirit behind it was jealousy. I was shocked when I started getting calls from major Christian leaders asking me if the tape was true! There were actually very few Christian leaders at the time that seemed to discern what was behind this attack.

The accusing pastor then put out a book of over one hundred eighty pages filled with accusations. I was with Mike Bickle, the pastor of KCF, when he received the book with the charges. We read much of it together, and it was hard for me to contain the anger I felt. Mike did not seem to be angry at all. Finally, out of the hundreds of false charges, Mike found a couple that he felt were true and said he needed to publicly repent of those. I was shocked and asked him about the multitude of false charges, and if he was going to answer those. His response was that pride had entered into their movement, providing a great opportunity for the Kansas City Fellowship to humble themselves, and he did not want to miss it.

I greatly appreciated Mike's response to this persecution. He was forearmed, as they had been told prophetically years before that this attack was coming and who it would come through. Mike's determination not to defend their ministry, but to embrace the humility, was the right one for his church I think. They were not doing everything perfectly, and they were constantly revealing mistakes they had made in trying to shepherd some of the remarkable gifts that were in their midst. However, it is my opinion that the church as a whole in America missed a great visitation by not handling this thing right and defending KCF against the false charges.

Time Alone Does Not Heal

By bringing this up now, some will think that I am just stirring up old wounds that need to be covered and forgotten. However, wounds do not heal with time, but become infected if they are not treated correctly. This terrible wound on the body of Christ in America was never treated correctly. I will continue to point to it for as long as it goes untreated. The ones that I irritate the most by this are probably the ones who need to wake up and to do their job, if indeed they are true elders in the body. Jealousy was used to inflict this terrible wound, and it must be recognized and repented of, including the failure of the leaders to do their job of judging rightly. Otherwise, we will just continue to be open to the same kinds of attacks.

We must never forget that righteousness and justice are the foundation of the Lord's throne. The Apostle Paul wrote to the Corinthian church that it was to their shame that there were no judges among them. This has possibly cost the body of Christ more shame than any other thing. In the Old Testament, the elders sat in the gates as judges. The New Testament church government was taken from this model, yet it is hard to find a true elder who is willing to judge matters in the church. We will not have true church government until this happens.

Because there is a void left by those who are called as elders, but who fail to do their job as judges, many who are not called to this appoint themselves to be judges, and justice is even more perverted. The remarkable thing is that so much of the body of Christ will listen to those who obviously have jealousy dripping from their accusations. People whom I would not allow to oversee a home group can now acquire the attention of thousands just by putting something on the Internet. So many Christians accept their false accusations as being true just because they are written.

This truly reveals the state of protection the church now has from its shepherds and watchmen—not much. Jealousy should be one of the easiest evils to discern, yet it parades itself without challenge through much of the church. This must change. If we are called to be shepherds, or watchmen, and we do not warn the sheep of such blatant attacks by the accuser, then we have allowed the Lord's sheep to be freely attacked because of our negligence.

If jealousy has a place in our hearts, it will do evil to others, as well as to ourselves. The reason we are studying each of these works of the flesh is so that we can get free of them. We need to get free of them personally and as a church. The first thing we should do with each one is ask the Holy Spirit to reveal to us any evil thing which is in our own hearts, and honestly embrace what He shows us. Then repent by rejecting it, and resolving to pray and do good for any whom we may have jealousy in our hearts toward. As Robin McMillan experienced, rejecting jealousy can be the path to our own promotion and blessing. We must start recognizing jealousy, and not give it a place in our lives or the life of the church.

The Greek word translated **"jealousy"** in our text is *dichostsis,* which is also translated "division" and "sedition." As is becoming obvious as we study them, these works of the flesh are all related and tend to overlap each other. About half of those listed here all work toward the same evil end—the division of God's people from one another. We can count on righteous judges arising to expose, confront, and remove these deadly evils from the church before we will be able to fully accomplish our purpose in these times. The same is true for us individually. Don't miss your purpose— look for any signs of jealousy in your heart, repent, and get rid of it. Then reject it when it seeks to gain entry into the church.

OUTBURSTS OF ANGER

The next work of the flesh noted in Galatians 5:20 is **"outbursts of anger."** Today we would call this "losing your temper," "going ballistic," or "rage." Losing control of our anger is a work of the flesh, and like all works of the flesh, it will be used as an open door or a "gate of hell" by the devil. Our rage will hurt other people, as well as their respect for us.

Loose Cannons Will Never Be Trusted

Most people know at least one person who tries to control others with their anger. Few things can be more cruel or demeaning for the one who tries to do this, or for the ones who are subjected to it. Is that the kind of dignity that we would expect from someone who truly has authority, especially one who is an ambassador of the King of kings? Would the Lord ever behave that way? Could anyone who is led by the Holy Spirit behave that way? That is why being "quick-tempered" is listed with the other sins and personal problems which will disqualify one from being an elder in the church, as we read in Titus 1:7. Those who cannot control their tempers are, at best, still in bondage to the works of the flesh, and must not be appointed as leaders in the church.

Should those who lose their tempers immediately be removed from any position of authority in the church? This is a possibility simply because unrighteous anger is a very serious matter and can be a major open door for the devil to attack God's people. However, the work of the flesh listed in Galatians 5:20, **"outbursts of anger,"** is plural and refers to more than an isolated occurrence. Everyone has bad days and can be caught off guard when they are very tired or stressed, though any loss of control of our anger should be considered serious. We are more concerned about seeing a pattern. Is that the normal way this person deals with problems or stress? If the answer is yes, we do have a problem that should disqualify them from leadership in the church until it is overcome.

When Slow Is Good

In James 1:19-20, we are told: **"...but let everyone be quick to hear, slow to speak and slow to anger; for the anger of man does not achieve the righteousness of God."** This is another reason why an elder cannot be one who is prone to being quick-tempered. An angry, quick-tempered person can intimidate people into submission out of fear, but his anger will never change their hearts. God does not just want us doing the right things; He wants us to do them because righteousness, or doing right, is in our hearts. The devil tries to control others through intimidation and fear. God imparts truth that sets people free, and He draws us with His love.

This does not mean we can never get angry or that God does not at times get angry. His anger can grow into wrath, as the world has seen often, and will yet experience. There are limits to His patience and His mercy, and once those limits are crossed, He does release His wrath. However, at no time does He lose control of His anger, and His response in His anger is righteous and just.

We are told in Proverbs 16:32, **"He who is slow to anger is better than the mighty, and he who rules his spirit, than he who captures a city."** The ability to rule our emotions so that we never lose our tempers is one of the surest signs of true wisdom, maturity, and great spiritual strength. This is required for anyone who would be a leader in the church, but we should also look for it in those who would be given authority in anything.

In Ephesians 4:26-27 we are told, **"Be angry, and yet do not sin; do not let the sun go down on your anger, and do not give the devil an opportunity."** To be angry is not a sin if it is for the right reasons. However, to lose control of our anger is, regardless of the reason. One reason that many lose control of their anger is because they **"let the sun go down."** They harbor it for long periods of time and it builds up like steam in a boiler. If there is not a relief valve on a boiler, it will become a bomb capable of much destruction. The same is true of our anger.

This is usually the reason why parents lose their tempers with their children. Many parents teach their children that they really do not mean "no" until they have said it a number of times and raised their voice to a certain decibel level. They allow their children to keep pressuring them and then often give into the pressure. This is one of the most harmful things we can do to our children, and it can negatively affect them their whole lives. This is evil, as the Lord said in Matthew 5:37, **"But let your 'Yes' be 'Yes,' and your 'No,' 'No.' For whatever is more than these is from the evil one"** (NKJV).

As a manager, business owner, and now leader of a ministry, I become aware very quickly of any person who cannot follow instructions or who has to be reminded of them repeatedly. I may not fire that person for this, but in many positions, I would. At best, they will always be limited in the authority or responsibility that I can trust them with. In some, I may see enough other good qualities to try and work with them in this, and I may feel compassion knowing that it was poor parenting that caused it in some. But they still cannot be trusted except to the degree that they can follow instructions and do not need oversight to ensure this.

If we teach our children that our "yes" or "no" is exactly what we mean the first time, they will not be prone to try to pressure and manipulate us into changing our minds. This does not mean there can be no room for appeal, but if we allow our children to badger and nag because they learn that it can cause us to give into their will in the matter, we are, at best, being negligent in our duties as parents to teach them obedience. Worse, we are most likely building up a frustration that will boil over into a rage at some point. The key is to teach our children to obey us the first time we give an instruction, and that our "yes" and "no" really do mean exactly that.

Of course, there have been books written on anger management, and the subject is certainly worthy of a book. How much of the death and destruction the world has suffered has been the result of this one problem? Think about it. Uncontrolled anger does destroy, to at least some degree, every time it is released. It is therefore paramount that anyone in any leadership position in the church be free from this terrible demonic inroad.

Keeping away from strife is an honor for a man, but any fool will quarrel (Proverbs 20:3).

A fool always loses his temper, but a wise man holds it back (Proverbs 29:11).

CHAPTER TEN

A DISAGREEABLE SPIRIT

The next "work of the flesh" noted in Galatians 5:20 is **"disputes,"** or as it is called in some translations, **"strife" (KJV).** This is having a contrary, disagreeable spirit. All of these works of the flesh are interconnected, and they feed and set up one another in many different ways. Worse than that, the devil feeds on them! How?

Dust and the Carnal Nature

The Lord condemned the serpent to crawl on his belly and eat the dust. Because the flesh of man was made from the dust, this was a prophetic statement of how the devil would feed on the carnal nature of man. This is why the devil promotes this carnality and sinful nature—it feeds him! Every time we give into one of the works of the flesh, it is feeding the very devils that are seeking to bind us and use us for their own evil purposes.

Because being at peace is fundamental to abiding in the Lord, who is the Prince of Peace, causing strife and disputes is a fundamental strategy of the devil to keep us from abiding in Him. We can all probably think of people we have known who are prone to dispute almost any statement they hear. Those who have this problem, which is a serious character flaw as are all of the other works of the flesh, will often argue with others even if they agree with them! Those who are prone to do this may make good lawyers, challenging everything they hear to test the validity of the statements, but outside of a courtroom those who do this are very difficult to be around and can be disruptive to any group, team, or organization.

This tendency to be argumentative can make intelligent, informative, and constructive conversation very difficult if they are around. In an organization, such people can make constructive advancement difficult. These are the types of people that good management courses will teach you to identify and either isolate or get rid of. They can be like the proverbial rotten apple that spoils the whole barrel. The Lord seems to feel the same way about keeping them away from His business.

This does not mean that there should not be room for disagreements or challenging statements, positions, or propositions. There is often a need for this so that we examine things more deeply or carefully. However, there is a difference in someone doing this for the sake of a deeper examination, and someone who is just argumentative. The latter is a work of the flesh, and it will not help lead us to righteousness, but will rather be prone to cause destructive divisions.

How to Save Friends

Now, after thinking of someone you know who is like this, almost certainly someone that you do not like being around—consider for a moment if this could possibly be the way others see you. Just about every time I hear a very convicting sermon or word, I start thinking of people whom I wish could hear this, and the Lord has to remind me that He has me there listening to it, not them! Before we ever go looking for the splinters in other people's eyes, let us be sure that we do not have a log in our own.

For some reason if I do not like a person, have been hurt or rejected by them, or am just irritated with them at the time, I will be far more prone to want to challenge or reject anything they say. Likewise, if I have recently been blessed by someone in some way, I am far more prone to listen openly to what they are saying. However, one of the important lessons I learned the first year I was a Christian is that the people I may tend to want to reject the most are often the ones who have the very wisdom, knowledge, or perspective that I need the most. I know now that if I want to learn something, I need to humble myself and listen to those who I might not be prone to listen to.

Could this be why the Lord sent Peter to the Jews and Paul to the Gentiles? It seems that the opposite would have worked better. The Jews would have identified with and more easily listened to Paul rather than Peter. Paul was a disciple of the esteemed teacher,

Gamaliel, and a "Pharisee of Pharisees," while Peter was an unlearned fisherman and common man whom the Jews tended to have a basic disrespect for. It seems that the Gentiles would have listened to a person like Peter more easily than Paul, whose strict religious nature was an affront to them. However, the Jews did not need what was in Peter's head, but rather what was in his heart. Likewise, the Gentiles needed the systematic and sound teaching which Paul excelled in. Both groups had to humble themselves to get what they needed, and grace is required to receive the grace of God. Both Peter and Paul were cast in a humble dependency on the Holy Spirit to accomplish their purposes, because everything in the natural was against them.

My point is that those who are prone to be argumentative will be poor learners. Though they usually assume they know more than others, or can reason better than others, such individuals are usually the most foolish people of all, and accomplishing little or nothing in their lives. Almost all accomplishments require a team of people to get the job done, and this spirit is destructive on any team. These are the critical, cynical people who feel that it is their place in life to attack and expose others. This cynicism has invaded and perverted modern journalism in a way that directly undercuts the path to real truth and faith, which begins with humility and openness.

This does not mean that we accept everything we hear without examining it, but as Paul exhorted in I

Thessalonians 5:21, **"But examine everything carefully; hold fast to that which is good."** This implies testing what we hear by looking for the good, not the bad. There is a difference. When we look at something with positive expectations, which is in faith, we will be far more open to seeing it accurately than if we look at it through the eyes of doubt. Because we have faith, it does not mean that we reject discernment; we know how to recognize that which is not true. However, those who doubt and have eyes that are already half-closed, will miss the truth they could have received far more often than those who have positive expectations.

Many Christians are now cynical because they have been hurt or disappointed by other Christians or churches. I was recently talking to someone who was very proud of being so "discerning" that he could not be fooled again. But there was such a darkness of heart toward people, especially God's people, that this person was not close to anyone, nor could be. Even while talking to him I wanted to get as far away from him as I could. I started thinking that I would rather be continually deceived and hurt by people than to lose my love for them. I think God would prefer this also.

Love Is Defenseless

Do you think when we are standing before the judgment seat of Christ that He is going to commend us for all of the times that we discerned that a person was going to hurt us or deceive us in some way, so we rejected them before they had the chance? I think we are far more likely to be commended for the times we were hurt, or used wrongly by others, and forgave them, and by the trial even grew in love and the fruit of the Spirit. True love will always be open to being hurt, but it will never throw up a protective barrier or it would not be true love.

If we are prone to "disputes" or being argumentative, we are either proud fools who are unteachable or we are wounded. People in this condition are not able to grow in love. Just as Jesus, who is the Truth, had to be hurt and crucified by the very ones He came to save in order to save them, if we have ceased to be hurt by anyone, we have probably stopped walking in the kind of love that leads others to the salvation of the cross. We must bear the cross to lead others to it.

So, to be free of this destructive work of the flesh, let us learn to recognize the opportunity to love people, and may we grow in patience when we hear them say things we do not think are true. Before challenging them, consider best how to do it with the utmost respect and dignity, which will open them up to hear what we have to say. You can win arguments but lose friends. We do not want to compromise truth and integrity, but we must seek to stand for truth and integrity in the way that will more easily open others up to the truth.

CHAPTER ELEVEN

SEDITION

The next work of the flesh noted in Galatians 5:20 is **"seditions"** (KJV). This word also means "rebellion" or "division." Its implication is more than just resisting authority. It is also to incite others to rebel or turn against authority. This is, of course, what almost all rebellion eventually does.

Rebellion Kills Its Friends

Rebellion is a sin that rarely stands alone, and it will cause others to stumble as well, just as when Satan rebelled and a third of the angels fell with him. That is why this particular work of the fallen nature is so destructive as to repeatedly warrant the Lord's most severe response. One of the most spectacular events of that journey was the result of Korah's rebellion, in which the very earth itself opened and swallowed all who had joined the rebellion.

That the Lord would take such a drastic measure with this rebellion was not just a reflection of His anger, but the need for extreme measures in dealing with sedition, because it is so easily spread to many others and will, therefore, spread the destruction to more of His people.

Like all of these other works of the flesh, we usually do not have to look far to find examples of this in the church. A rebellious person will almost always seek to gain converts to his rebellion, because the more people in agreement with the sin, the more justified he feels about it. However, our sin is multiplied with every convert we make, and the ultimate end of the matter will be even more tragic for those who become seditious, or lead others to rebellion.

To grasp just how much the Lord hates this particular sin, let's look at Numbers 16. I will only pull out some of the highlights of this chapter, but it can be beneficial to read it in its entirety.

> **Now Korah. . .rose up before Moses, together with some of the sons of Israel, two hundred and fifty leaders of the congregation, chosen in the assembly, men of renown.**
>
> **And they assembled together against Moses and Aaron, and said to them, "You have gone far enough, for all the congregation are holy, every one of them, and the Lord is in their midst; so why do you exalt yourselves above the assembly of the Lord?"**
>
> **When Moses heard this, he fell on his face (Numbers 16:1-4).**
>
> **Then Moses said to Korah, "Hear now, you sons of Levi,**

is it not enough for you that the God of Israel has separated you from the rest of the congregation of Israel, to bring you near to Himself, to do the service of the tabernacle of the Lord, and to stand before the congregation to minister to them?" (Numbers 16:8-9)

Thus Korah assembled all the congregation against them at the doorway of the tent of meeting. And the glory of the Lord appeared to all the congregation.

Then the Lord spoke to Moses and Aaron, saying,

"Separate yourselves from among this congregation, that I may consume them instantly."

But they fell on their faces, and said, "O God, Thou God of the spirits of all flesh, when one man sins, wilt Thou be angry with the entire congregation?"

Then the Lord spoke to Moses, saying,

"Speak to the congregation, saying, 'Get back from around the dwellings of Korah, Dathan, and Abiram'" (Numbers 16:19-24).

Then it came about as he finished speaking all these words, that the ground that was under them split open;

and the earth opened its mouth and swallowed them up, and their households, and all the men who belonged to Korah, with their possessions.

So they and all that belonged to them went down alive to Sheol; and the earth closed over them, and they perished from the midst of the assembly.

And all Israel who were around them fled at their outcry, for they said, "The earth may swallow us up!"

Fire also came forth from the Lord and consumed the two hundred and fifty men who were offering the incense (Numbers 16:31-35).

The point of this is that Korah did not just rebel himself, but he incited a rebellion. Such behavior will have the most terrible consequences in the end.

Rebellion Is Never the Answer

It seems that if anyone in Scripture had a cause to rebel against his authority it was David in relation to Saul. Saul had not only killed the priests of the Lord, but was unjustly trying to kill David. Yet, how did David respond to this? David could have killed Saul with the Lord's permission. The Lord had told David that He was going to deliver his enemy into his hand, and he could do to Saul whatever he wanted. However,

David's heart smote him for just cutting off the hem of Saul's robe because this meant he had touched the Lord's anointed.

David could have killed Saul and become king right then, which would have been a fulfillment of a prophecy given to him. However, David would have likely died in the same way, because we reap what we sow. By patiently waiting for the Lord to remove Saul, the one He had placed in authority, and waiting for the Lord to establish himself, David established a throne which would last forever, which even Jesus is now seated upon.

David was willing to serve the house of Saul, and he did, continually honoring Saul, even after his death. David did this because of his respect for authority. Those who understand truth, integrity, and the ways of the Lord will never try to gain influence or a position by sedition. Those who do are only sealing their own doom and are sure to experience the same kind of rebellion against them. Just because there is unrighteous authority, it never justifies unrighteous rebellion to remove it.

CHAPTER TWELVE

HERESIES

The next work of the flesh noted in Galatians 5:20 is translated **"heresies,"** or **"factions."** We often relate heresy to teaching a false doctrine, but a heresy is actually creating a division, or faction, in the church. Of course false teachings will do this, but one can also use the truth to be divisive and contentious.

There are people who are divisive and will use almost anything to bring divisions. Factions have been created in churches over even the most trifling matters, but whether factions are created over something major or minor does not matter—it is a work of the flesh, and it is evil.

The Worst Judgment

A main theme of the Book of Jude is to recognize and watch out for those who **"cause divisions" (see verse 19).** Here they are described as being like reefs are to ships; they stay hidden and operate with subtlety, but they do great damage to believers. As this Book also states, these are the ones that the worst judgment is being reserved for. Without question, bringing divisions to the body of Christ is one of the worst transgressions we can be involved in. In Proverbs 6:16-19, we are told that one of the seven things that the Lord hates is bringing strife among brothers.

His Greatest Desire

As we discussed previously, if you knew that you were going to die tomorrow, your prayers would become very real and focused on the things that mean the most to you. Therefore, we can assume that the Lord's Prayer the night before He was crucified reflected the things that were the deepest issues of His heart. Sown throughout that great prayer recorded in John 17, to the degree that it could be considered the main theme of that prayer, was the Lord's heart for the unity of His people, as He stated in verse 11.

> **"And I am no more in the world; and yet they themselves are in the world, and I come to Thee. Holy Father, keep them in Thy name, the name which Thou hast given Me, that they may be one, even as We are."**

When we look at the present state of the church, it is understandable that many would consider a true unity of the church impossible. However, nothing is impossible for God, and we can be assured that the prayer of Jesus is going to be answered! Those who truly love Him love the things that He loves and are devoted to seeing His will done on the earth. Therefore, the unity of His people should be one of the primary devotions of every Christian. We must also consider that here the Lord does not just pray for our unity, but for us to have the same kind of unity that He has with the Father!

Though we can be sure that the prayer of Jesus is going to be answered, and that this will most certainly one day come to pass, if we are wise, we, too, will begin to pray for this. Why should we pray if Jesus has already prayed and we know that it is going to come to pass? Intercession is not just for the purpose of getting God to do things for us, but it is also for the purpose of aligning our hearts with God's heart. The more we have invested in the unity of the body of Christ through the prayers we have made, the more our hearts will be devoted to it.

When Daniel read in the prophecy of Jeremiah that the exile would be seventy years, and he calculated that the time was up, he did not just start rejoicing that his people would soon return and rebuild Jerusalem; he started interceding for God's Word to come to pass. We should always do the same when we discern God's will in a matter.

In John 17:20-21, the Lord added to His reason for desiring the unity of His people when He prayed:

> **"I do not ask in behalf of these alone, but for those also who believe in Me through their word;**
>
> **that they may all be one; even as Thou, Father, art in Me, and I am in Thee, that**

they also may be in Us; that the world may believe that Thou didst send Me."

One of the reasons why the Lord prayed for our unity is **"that they also may be in Us."** This indicates that the way that we abide in the Lord is by being in unity with one another. Indeed, this has to be true. How could someone truly be in unity with the Head without also being in unity with His body? The truest evidence that we have come to abide in Him will be our unity with one another.

Then the Lord gives us another crucial reason for this—when this unity comes, the whole world will believe that Jesus was sent by the Father. From the time there were just two brothers on the earth, they could not get along, and one of them killed the other. Fighting among people has been the constant state of the world since the Fall. Therefore, when true unity among the people who follow Jesus is observed, it will be an unquestionable miracle to all of the people who live on the earth. This will cause them to know for sure that Jesus really was sent by God. Therefore, the greatest evangelistic power on the earth is the unity of the church.

In verse 22 of this great chapter, the Lord gives us an insight as to how this unity will come:

"And the glory which Thou hast given Me I have given to them; that they may be one, just as We are one."

The body of Christ will never come into unity around a doctrine or church government, although these things are important. Even so, the way His people are going to come into unity is by seeing His glory. When the Lamb entered, even the twenty-four elders fell down and cast their crowns at His feet. Who could presume glory or position, or maintain divisions in the presence of the Lamb?

I have had a few experiences when I saw the glory of God manifested together with a group of people. Not only were all of the petty differences I may have had with these people immediately shown to be as petty as they were, but somehow we were all bonded together in a very special way because we had seen the glory of God together. I am often asked how the core team of our ministry has stayed together for so many years. I can answer that easily—it is because we have experienced the glory of God together.

In John 17:23, the Lord adds yet another insight into the reason unity is so crucial for His people:

"I in them, and Thou in Me, that they may be perfected in unity, that the world may know that Thou didst send Me, and didst love them, even as Thou didst love Me."

We are called "the body of Christ." Think about it: Will any part of your body enter into its full purpose without the rest of your body? Because we must be **"perfected in unity,"** none of us can expect to enter into our own full purpose without the rest of the body of Christ. Therefore, if for no other reason than selfish ones, we should do all that we can to help bring unity to the body of Christ. We should also resist and recognize divisions as the great evil that they are—anything or anyone that causes division in His church.

CHAPTER THIRTEEN

ENVY

The next work of the flesh we will study from Galatians 5:21 is **"envying."** This is similar to **"jealousy,"** which we studied previously, but it is a little different. Jealousy is more directed at a person, while envy is directed more at possessions or positions. Though all of these works of the flesh are to some degree intertwined and overlapping, the apostle listed them separately for an obvious reason, and so we should look for their distinguishing characteristics.

The Source of Persecution

Like jealousy, envy is one of the most deadly of these evil works, and we are told that even Jesus was crucified because of envy (see Matthew 27:18, Mark 15:10). The Pharisees and Sadducees were envious of the great crowds that followed the Lord. The envious will rarely have anyone following them who is not somehow forced to, so they will be prone to win followers by attacking others. This, too, is where many of the divisions and infighting in the body of Christ begin.

When one church in a place starts to grow and prosper, or a special grace or anointing comes upon it, church history testifies that this will likely result in persecution from other churches. This is a deadly trap that has ruined the otherwise good service of many church leaders. It is the same evil that caused the leaders of Israel to fall in the first century and reject their Messiah.

Envy can be destructive in any form, doing damage to any relationship, but envy between church leaders can be one of the most destructive of all of the works of the flesh. This is because when it is manifested in leaders it will infect their followers, defiling many people and bringing devastating enmities and divisions in the church. These leaders will usually claim to be protecting the sheep or defending the truth, but the Lord is not fooled, and we must not continue to be either. You will find at the root of almost every division in the body of Christ either jealousy or envy. We must learn to recognize these evils when they arise in our own hearts or in those we accept as our leaders.

Protect Your Leaders

When we see this arising in our leaders, we have a responsibility to speak to them about it. It should be done in gentleness and with respect, but it must be done. If they are not teachable or able to receive such correction from other people, they should not be leaders in the church anyway. However, I know of cases where very good men or women of God had their ministries saved by members of their flocks who cared enough for them to confront them when they saw them heading for such a fall.

As the Lord taught in the Parable of the Sheep and Goats in Matthew 25:40, **"Truly I say to you, to the extent that you did it to one of these brothers of Mine, even the least of them, you did it to Me."** Therefore, if we are envious or jealous of any of His people and thereby persecute them, we are actually being envious of the Lord Himself and are persecuting Him. The way that we treat His people, even **"the least of them,"** is the way that we are treating the Lord.

One of the most tragic ways that envy has manifested itself in church history has been the way a passing generation tends to persecute the emerging generation. Instead of blessing them and helping them prepare for their own purpose, they become envious and begin to attack them. Just as King Saul became envious of David, those who are insecure in their position will be threatened by any new movements or ministries that emerge and often attack them. This has been repeated in almost every spiritual generation to date.

The worst curse that was ever placed on Israel was that if they forsook the Lord, they would end up devouring their own young. One could say that this seems to be exactly what has happened to almost every generation in church history. To date, any new movement that is raised up to bring an advance in the restoration of truth or life to the church will suffer its greatest threat from its own spiritual parents.

It is easy for a subtle form of pride to come upon those who are mightily used by the Lord, which would cause them to think that if the Lord desires to do anything new or great on the earth, He would certainly call on them first. Many who have been used by the Lord have fallen to this pride which actually disqualifies them from further use by the Lord. Since they believe they are the best candidates for accomplishing any major purpose of the Lord, they cannot conceive that any such thing that comes through others could, therefore, be from the Lord, so they reject it and often persecute it.

An Ultimate Unity

There will be a time when the hearts of the fathers and sons are united, and then we will know that the end of this age is truly near, just as we are told in the last chapter of Malachi. Until then, we need to understand that those who arise with a special anointing or grace for leadership of a new emerging church or movement will most likely be attacked by the present church leadership. Again, this will almost always be done in the name of "protecting the sheep," or "defending the truth," but without question, the real reason is almost always envy.

One reason why so many church leaders seem prone to this is that most pastors live in a very tenuous place. It may be one of the most insecure jobs one can have on the planet. Most congregations are small, and the budgets of the churches and their pastors very tight, so that losing just a few people can be a threat to both their church and ministry. When one highly visible leader recently began a church in one American city, it was said that over one hundred twenty small churches there immediately closed. Many of these were faithful shepherds and warriors who really were on the frontlines of the battle between light and darkness in that city for many hard years, and instantly they were out of a job.

Spiritual Cancer

Just as any organ in the body that begins to grow without regard to the rest of the body is cancerous, any church that grows without regard for the rest of the body is cancerous. If we do not want to be a cancer to the body, we must always be considerate of the rest of the body. Even so, it is a most grievous thing to see many who have run well for their whole lives fall to this kind of envy near the end of their lives, even if it is because their life's work is threatened.

As I am getting older, I have been more interested in understanding this and have concluded that it is often because they have not been healed of the afflictions that others brought upon them, which is simply the failure to forgive. Unforgiveness leads to bitterness, and bitterness will defile or poison many others. Because we are a ministry that is almost continually attacked by someone, we have to preach, teach, and practice forgiveness continually. Even though I think we have done fairly well so far, I know that we could fall at the end of our journey and not have a truly successful journey. This is hard, but it is also our best opportunity to be transformed into the Lord's image. Isn't forgiveness the basis of the New Covenant? Isn't that the main message of the cross? We therefore must keep it as a main practice in our lives.

There is a pastor in the Charlotte area that seems to have built his ministry on just attacking us. I was listening to his radio broadcast one time, and he was saying many things that were not true about us (and some that were). Being provoked, I asked the Lord if He would stop this man. The Lord replied instantly, "Yes, but who do you want to take his place?"

I got the point and have been content to let this man continue attacking us for many years now. I think it may continue through him and others until we have been conformed to the image of the Lord, who laid down His own life for the very ones who were torturing Him. Since we obviously still have quite a way to go to be like Him, I expect this to continue until that transformation is complete. I, therefore, do not want to run from such attacks, but welcome them as the opportunity they are.

Another way we have tried to combat this tendency to be envious or jealous of others is to give positions of authority in our ministry only to those who show a genuine devotion to equipping and raising up others. One of the main things I look for in leaders is the joy on their faces when those under them do well. Our key leaders all tend to get more excited about those whom they have trained being used by God in a major way than they do when they are personally used by God. These are true spiritual fathers and mothers who are deserving of "double honor."

Paul the Apostle observed that we have many teachers but not many fathers, and I think the same is still true (see I Corinthians 4:15). We tend to call spiritual fathers those who are older and experienced, but being a father has nothing to do with age or experience, rather it has much to do with the ability to reproduce. Just as in the natural, most become fathers when they are rather young, and the true equipping ministries that are listed in Ephesians 4 may also be quite young. There are many who do ministry well, but rarely train or equip others. We need to question whether such ministries are really the equipping ministries listed in Ephesians 4, as their primary purpose is to equip others to do the work of the ministry.

True Fathers and Mothers

The greatest parents in the natural all want their children to do better than they did, and rejoice when they do. The same is true spiritually. When we begin to take this calling to equip others seriously, knowing that this will be the only way that the church can attain **"...unity of the faith, and of the knowledge of the Son of God, to a mature man, to the measure of the stature which belongs to the fulness of Christ" (Ephesians 4:13).**

We should try to keep as the focus of our lives the ultimate reward of success in this life, which is to hear the Lord say on that great day, **"Well done, good and faithful servant" (Matthew 25:21 NIV)**. As a pastor I also realize that for me to hear those greatest words, I must do all I can to ensure that those the Lord has entrusted to my care hear the same words. Therefore, I must keep in mind that my hope of success is the success of those who are a part of our ministry and the members of our churches. Because of this, I am compelled to measure my success by how well others are accomplishing their purpose.

If we truly see that a basic measure of our own success is the growing anointing and success of those we have trained, it is much harder to be envious of them. For this reason I believe that John the Baptist is one of the greatest examples of true godly leadership. His whole job was to point to Jesus and to prepare the way for Him, not just build his own following. He knew all along that the One coming to follow him was much greater, and he considered himself not even worthy to untie His shoes. Then, when the anointed One came, he rejoiced just to hear His voice, being a true friend of the Bridegroom. He also rejoiced to decrease as Jesus increased. For this reason, John was honored by the Lord as being called the greatest man born of a woman. Such true nobility of spirit is the hallmark of those who truly are the greatest.

CHAPTER FOURTEEN

DRUNKENNESS

The next work of the flesh we will study from Galatians 5:21 is **"drunkenness."** Of course, getting drunk, or high, should have no place in the life of a Christian. To become drunk is to, at best, reduce your ability to control yourself or to resist the devil. When this happens, we can count on the other works of the flesh to assert themselves, and the devil will take advantage to do his evil work to us or through us.

A Moment Can Kill

There are many people who have paid the price for the rest of their lives because of one event while drunk. A drunk driver may have never meant to hurt anyone, but many people are dead, and many others are crippled for life because of drunk drivers. Many of these were innocent children. Those drunk drivers also had their own lives devastated, and many permanently ruined, by one foolish lapse in judgment because they allowed themselves to become drunk.

Others have said or done things when they were drunk for which they will be sorry for the rest of their lives. Most of these were sure that they could control themselves while drinking. But the more that is drunk, the more control that is lost, and you can count on what happens then not to be positive. Anyone who becomes drunk is inviting the devil to take his best shot, and he will rarely fail to take advantage of such an opportunity.

Before I became a Christian, I would sometimes try to get my dates drunk, for obvious reasons. If I was able to get them drunk, I would lose respect for them and never take them seriously. I simply did not trust them enough to become serious if they were able to lose control of themselves like that. The same was true with almost every guy I knew. I watched many serious relationships break up because of this. We think we are being cool, and people can laugh at us when we are drunk, but at the same time they are losing their respect for us, regardless of how much they may say otherwise.

Losing Their Trust

When I was in the Navy, I did my share of carousing and drinking. However, I was also very aware of any of my squadron friends or shipmates who drank too much and lost control while on liberty. I may have continued to like them after that, but I would never trust them with important secrets, information, or responsibility if they worked with me. If someone allows themselves to become drunk, they simply are not trustworthy.

Of course, many believers have interpreted this to mean that we should never touch wine or any other alcoholic drink. When we see the devastation and harm to so many people because of alcohol, it is easy to understand this resolve not to touch alcohol. However, that is not a biblical teaching or perspective. Nowhere does the Bible command abstinence from alcoholic drink, though it does have a great deal to say about excessive drinking or drunkenness.

Those who have tried to condemn any drinking of alcohol by calling it a biblical doctrine have to substantially bend the Scriptures to come up with that. This is a serious transgression itself and is considered by many theologians to be the open door through which Satan was able to deceive Eve in the Garden.

Adding to the Word

The Lord had commanded them not to eat from the Tree of the Knowledge of Good and Evil, but when asked what God had told Eve, she replied that they could not eat from it or touch it (see Genesis 3:3). The Lord had not said anything about touching the tree. Her tendency to add to what God had said in this way revealed a basic disrespect for His Word that the devil was able to exploit. This is also what the Pharisees had done to the Law of Moses which made it of no effect, and soon made the traditions and precepts of men more the attention of the people than the Law itself.

In this same way, when people stretch or add to the Scriptures to justify their pet doctrines, it makes everyone who esteems the integrity of the Scriptures lose confidence or respect for them. Sadly, going to such an extreme, even with the noble motive of trying to protect people, has proven to not only be ineffective in doing that, but seems to even aggravate the problem. When our nation tried to force prohibition on everyone, the government may have had good intentions, but they so magnified the problems with alcohol that we have not yet fully recovered from this debacle.

It Doesn't Work

Studies have also repeatedly shown that the denominations which do not allow any drinking of alcohol have a higher percentage of alcoholics than those who do not condemn the drinking of alcohol. Interestingly, they also tend to have the highest rate of strokes and heart disease, which some studies indicate are also related. A very modest amount of wine with a meal does help digestion, as well as the circulatory system. This seems to be why the French, who almost all drink wine with their meals, tend to eat some of the richest food in the world, and yet have a very low rate of heart problems or strokes. Could this be why Paul the Apostle encouraged Timothy to drink a little wine for the sake of his stomach? (see I Timothy 5:23)

Studies also show that people groups who freely allow drinking in their culture, such as the Jews, tend to have a much lower incidence of alcoholics. I have spent a great deal of time in Europe over the last twenty years, yet I do not remember seeing a single drunk in public unless it was an American. The French, who freely drink wine with their meals, frown on drinking to excess, and are offended at the drinking of wine when it is not at a meal.

Now we do not want to base our doctrines on such studies, but on the Scriptures. However, these studies do seem to verify the sound teaching of the Scriptures that legalism is not the answer to lawlessness. Legalism is the result of people adding their own prejudices and opinions to the Scriptures, and turning them into commandments. Again, it was because of their practice of doing this that the Pharisees, who were seemingly the most devoted to the written Word of God, could not recognize God, the Word Himself, when He came to them.

If anyone has a problem with drinking to excess, then no alcoholic beverage should be drunk. If we are with someone who has a problem with drinking, we should not drink in their presence lest we cause them to stumble. That is the commandment of love. However, this is not a commandment that we can impose on others. To do so, especially if we try to imply that it is a biblical teaching, is to add to the Scriptures what you will never find in them.

Don't Be Foolish

The Lord Jesus not only drank wine, He made a lot of it with His first miracle. Some, who are not able to comprehend this because of their prejudice against drinking alcohol, have asserted that He drank grape juice and made grape juice at the wedding in Cana. Such assertions make those who hold to them appear foolish at best to anyone truly devoted to the integrity of Scripture or reason. The Greek word translated "wine" in these texts actually means "fermented grapes." There is no room for an honest person who seeks to be faithful to the Word of God, or to reason, to assert that Jesus only drank grape juice. Why would He then be accused of being "a wine bibber" or "a drunkard" if He was only drinking grape juice?

This kind of foolishness causes thinking people to assume that the Scriptures are full of contradictions. It is not the Scriptures, but people who are adding to the Word of God to try to establish as a doctrine what is in fact their own prejudice. Even so, we can be sure that the Lord never drank to excess or to a degree that it could affect His judgment, and neither would anyone who is led by the Spirit.

As the Lord Jesus Himself pointed out, because John the Baptist did not drink at all, people thought that he was eccentric. Because Jesus did drink wine, people accused Him of excess, though He obviously never drank to excess. People will accuse you and misunderstand you regardless of which side you take. However, as both John and Jesus revealed through their practices, among Christians there should be room for both positions without them accusing or misunderstanding each other.

One thing is certain, if you become drunk or high, the devil will use it against you and any others that he can. A single lapse here can cost you dearly for the rest of your life. It is not worth it. Why give the devil such a wide open opportunity to take a shot at you? Why would you want to do anything like this that could for any period of time compromise your sensitivity to and fellowship with the Holy Spirit? As Paul wrote in Ephesians 5:18: **"And do not get drunk with wine, for that is dissipation, but be filled with the Spirit."**

CHAPTER FIFTEEN

CAROUSING

The last of the works of the flesh that Paul lists in Galatians 5:21 is **"carousing."** This is more than just joking around. The Greek word translated as **"carousing"** implies being loud and foolish. This is because the carnal nature is prone to being self-centered and likes to be the center of attention. The more we let the carnal nature exert itself, the louder and more boisterous it often becomes. This is contrary to the kingdom of God because the most basic devotion of the Holy Spirit will always be to draw attention to the Son of God, not ourselves.

This does not mean that Christians should not have a personality or joke around and have a good time. However, there is a certain dignity and respect, which children of the King should conduct themselves. The true Christian nature is also one that serves and edifies others, even using humor to bless others rather than just draw attention to ourselves.

The Boisterous Are Self-Centered

Being boisterous in a way that is intended to just draw attention to ourselves may still seem to be a rather mild work of the flesh and hardly something worthy of condemning those who practice it as not being able to inherit the kingdom of God. However, this kind of behavior is but a symptom of a more basic character flaw that, if practiced, will steer most away from the Lord and His kingdom. True spiritual maturity is growing in the devotion to glorify the Lord, pointing to Him, not ourselves. If this nature of drawing attention to ourselves remains dominant, we will even use the gifts of the Holy Spirit in a way that promotes ourselves instead of the Lord. Possibly the ultimate form of profanity is to use that which is intended to inspire worship of God to draw attention to ourselves. This is what caused the fall of Satan himself.

It is also noteworthy that the English word "carousing" is the root word from which we derive "carousel," which means "to go in circles." There is a foolishness of spirit which may have us moving a lot, but in fact we are just going in circles and not making any true progress. Those who are prone to want to play all of the time, who measure the success of a gathering by how much fun was had, or how enjoyable it was for them personally, rarely make any progress toward true spiritual maturity.

The Mature Serve

In this same spirit, many Christians measure the value of a service or meeting by how they were touched. It should be our hope that everyone who attends any worship service be touched by God in some way. However, if that is all we are after, then we are still immature, or as Paul told the Corinthians, we are yet "carnal." The truly mature do not go to services in order to be touched, but rather to touch God, to worship and minister to Him, which is often done by serving His people. Remember: He said that as we did to the least of His we were doing to Him.

The temple does not exist for the people, but for the Lord. This does not mean that people are not to be ministered to in His temple, as they are His children, and to serve them is one way that we serve Him. But the greatest thing that anyone can do for themselves is to be lost in the worship and service of God, losing our own self-centeredness that is the deadly disease caused by the Fall.

What has been called "the Toronto Blessing" was a significant move of God in our time and was a blessing to those in the body of Christ who were open to it. After years of being devoted to teaching and hard work, many people did not need more teaching or more ministry as much as they needed a touch from God that let them know simply that they are loved by Him. Through this move, literally millions were personally touched by God in such a special way that they were convinced of this crucial truth. Even the most mature need affection from God, and this movement was like a big hug from God to His people.

There have been many interpretations offered about what the different characteristics of this unique move of God meant, but overall, it was almost like God tickling and playing with His children. Many, just by feeling God's personal affection for them, received healing and deliverance. Many were more profoundly changed by this than ten years worth of teaching could have accomplished.

Encounters Change

One basic truth that the Scriptures testify to over and over is that just one encounter with God will radically and profoundly change a person. When God Himself touches us, we will be different. That is why our primary pursuit must be God Himself, not just knowledge about Him. If we behold His glory with an unveiled face, we will be changed into His same image. The Toronto Blessing was, and continues to be, a touch from God that changes.

Tares Fake It

Even though I love what the Toronto Blessing imparted to the church, it was obvious that many people were faking being touched by God, and their foolishness brought some disrepute on that movement. Those who did this are a good example of what "carousing" means, as they were obviously just trying to bring attention to themselves.

Even so, this type of "carousing" has been common to every move of God, and God allows it just as He allows His enemy to sow tares in the midst of His wheat. Those who could only see the tares, and therefore shied away from the whole thing, missed a remarkable blessing. I will always be thankful for this movement. It is not at all surprising that this movement continues, though it may not be getting the same kind of attention that it once did. I expect it will continue in some form until the end of this age.

However, I also must confess, even after hours of being prayed for by many different people, I was never personally touched to the point of receiving even one holy giggle, much less "holy laughter." I did take a couple of "courtesy dives," falling down with the hope of maybe being touched on the way down, or while lying on the floor. I badly wanted to be touched, but it just never happened for me. However, I greatly enjoyed watching others get touched and loved watching it sweep through our church. Even more, I appreciated the fruit of that movement in drawing multitudes into a closer walk with the Lord.

There are some churches that have camped at this blessing, and I do not think that is necessarily a bad thing. It is important that there remain many places throughout the world where Christians can go for this special and powerful ministry. However, this is not the kind of ministry that most churches can build upon because it is not their calling. The ones who have been called to camp there have formed like a trail of oases through the wilderness for the sojourners, but most are meant to be sojourners and not stop moving until they get to the Promised Land.

A Mark of the Mature

Just as babies need constant attention from their parents, the more mature you become, the less attention you need. Christians who have to be continually reminded of God's affection for them by being touched in some way in every meeting are staying in a very immature state. Just as it is good, regardless of how old we are, to be encouraged and to experience the affection of our parents from time to time, all Christians can likewise use this ministry occasionally. However, those who camp at this one place are like those who get stuck at one oasis and do not finish their journey, going on to maturity.

As stated, the word "carouse" is the root word of "carousel." A carousel is a ride that goes around and around, gives you motion, and keeps you moving, but it does not really take you anywhere. There has been a fringe element that attached itself to the Toronto Blessing which seems to be on this spiritual carousel, moving a lot, but not really going anywhere spiritually. Many have judged the whole movement by these immature ones, but they were in fact just a small percentage of those who were ministered to by that great movement. The core of the movement itself has, in fact, had a very different devotion to moving on that is worthy of emulation.

There are those in probably every movement that are in it simply for their own benefit, and do not go on to maturity by seeking to be a blessing instead of just getting one. This is what we must guard our hearts against. There is a time for being touched and ministered to, and if we miss it we will usually become hard and cold Christians.

Never Reject Joy

The Toronto Blessing, and others like it, brought a badly needed warmth and joy to the church at just the right time, after years of facing major problems and the discipline of the Lord. It seemed as if, after the great spiritual spankings of the late 1980s, this was a big hug and affirmation from the Lord that He not only still loves us, but He loves us very much. In this same way, when my children were small and needed a lot of discipline, I tried to always give them much more affection than the discipline they received. As they got older, they did not need as much affirmation, but I still tried to keep the ratio weighted in favor of affection over correction. The Lord does the same. That is why He commanded much more feasting than fasting. He really is a very happy God.

Without question, the true Christian life is the most difficult life that you can live on this earth, but it is also the most fun, fulfilling, and exciting. By far the good part outweighs the hard. However, just as there is a time for joy, we will become eccentric if we do not also recognize the time for mourning, repenting, and grieving for our sins and the sins of others. To walk in truth, we must discern the seasons and timing of the Lord.

Now those who camp at the place of mourning and repentance, and fail to respond to the joy of the Holy Spirit when it comes, are usually the most sour and least attractive of all Christians. As we are told in Ecclesiastes 3, there are seasons for everything. If we do not recognize God's seasons, we will in fact be missing the major purposes of God in our time.

The Toronto Airport Christian Fellowship (TACF) remains a great oasis in the church where people can go when they need this and receive a genuine touch from God. This is a well that I pray will never get stopped up and will be used to raise up other similar churches and fellowships in every city. However, as stated, those who are moving on toward their inheritance will not camp long at any oasis. They get what they need and move on toward their purpose. We must realize when our people need such a break, but even though an oasis can be a wonderful place, we need to keep moving toward our ultimate calling. We have to also have the maturity to leave the comfort of an oasis and strike out across hard desert lands again.

It is impressive, and a wonderful example for us all, the way that the TACF became probably the main attraction in the body of Christ for a time, and yet were themselves always seeking to grow and add to their own fellowship what God was doing in other places. Probably a main reason why the Arnotts were chosen to lead in such an extraordinary way was their hunger and willingness to crisscross the earth to visit and receive from anyone that they thought had something special from God. That kind of hunger and humility is always rewarded. They received and did not just rejoice in their own blessing, but sought to immediately impart it to others as a blessing and enrichment to a huge part of the body of Christ.

Pressing On

The Brownsville Revival in Pensacola, Florida, was a similar visitation that imparted something very significant to much of the body of Christ. For this we should be thankful, but as we read in Amos 5:5-6 we are told, **"But do not resort to Bethel, and do not come to Gilgal, nor cross over to Beersheba; for Gilgal will certainly go into captivity, and Bethel will come to trouble. Seek the Lord that you may live...."** Gilgal, Bethel, and Beersheba were all places where the Lord had visited Israel (Jacob) in the past. Such places of great visitations usually make us go into bondage because people start worshiping the place God visited or the way God visited, instead of the God who visited. By its very definition, a visit is temporary. Even the great visitations of God in history were all temporary touches, and if you wanted to stay close to God, you needed to be ready to pick up and follow the cloud of His presence when He moved on.

Though we have not experienced anything on the level of the Toronto or Brownsville revivals yet, we have had a number of spectacular visitations in our churches and conferences. We have hundreds now on prophetic ministry teams who continue to astonish those who visit us with their gifts. People come from all over the world to receive ministry from them. I greatly appreciate the hunger of people who do this, and love the way the Lord touches them, but we will not have done our job if they have to keep coming to us rather than having such ministry raised up in their own cities and congregations. We hope to always be a well where people can receive this ministry. However, we know for the church to make it through the times ahead, there must be many others.

Many people seem surprised when they come to visit us and find that the prophetic ministry and gifts are not our primary focus. I think it was our focus for about two years out of the last two decades, but we, too, moved on. The prophetic ministry and gifts will probably and hopefully always be a ministry focus, and we will continue growing in them, but we are seeking to **"...grow up in all aspects into Him, who is the head, even Christ, from whom the whole body, being fitted and held together by that which every joint supplies, according to the proper working of each individual part, causes the growth of the body for the building up of itself in love" (Ephesians 4:15-16).** The prophetic is just one aspect of Him, and as great a blessing as the prophetic ministry can be, if we camp there, we, too, will just end up going in circles.

Carousing is not just having too much fun, but it is having fun that is self-centered, and it will result in our being on a carousel that really is not going anywhere. Such will keep us from the kingdom. Let us press on toward maturity, as the great Apostle wrote in Philippians 3:10-14:

that I may know Him, and the power of His resurrection and the fellowship of His sufferings, being conformed to His death;

in order that I may attain to the resurrection from the dead.

Not that I have already obtained it, or have already become perfect, but I press on in order that I may lay hold of that for which also I was laid hold of by Christ Jesus.

Brethren, I do not regard myself as having laid hold of it yet; but one thing I do: forgetting what lies behind and reaching forward to what lies ahead,

I press on toward the goal for the prize of the upward call of God in Christ Jesus.

Part II

The Fruit of the Spirit

CHAPTER SIXTEEN

FREEDOM

For you were called to freedom, brethren; only do not turn your freedom into an opportunity for the flesh, but through love serve one another.

For the whole Law is fulfilled in one word, in the statement, "You shall love your neighbor as yourself" (Galatians 5:13-14).

Before we begin to examine the fruit of the Spirit in some detail, there is a foundational principle of the kingdom that is essential for bearing true spiritual fruit—freedom. As we are told in II Corinthians 3:17, **"Now the Lord is the Spirit; and where the Spirit of the Lord is, there is liberty."** This could have also been translated, "where the Spirit is Lord there is liberty." Therefore, understanding freedom is crucial to understanding the kingdom, the domain where the Spirit is Lord, and the ground upon which the fruit of the Spirit is grown.

Freedom is not just the absence of bondage; it is the liberty to pursue all that we were created to be.

Those who use their freedom to do evil, or to do nothing, will end up back in bondage. True liberty is not static, but it is the freedom to pursue our purpose unhindered.

When Israel was set free from its bondage in Egypt, because of the toil they had suffered under for so long, many may have had a vision of a Promised Land where there was no labor at all. However, it would not be a very good place for long, and neither would they have remained free for long. Just as man was put in the Garden to cultivate it, man was created to labor, and even psychology has determined that any person will go insane if deprived of meaningful labor. However, there is a great difference between the toil of bondage and freedom to labor as we were created to do.

Liberty and Labor

Toil was the curse, but toil does not just mean hard labor, but difficult, painful, and stressful labor. Toil is a struggle, while labor as it was created to be, in harmony with our environment, will be exhilarating. Toil actually deprives us of who we are, while the labor of liberty sets us free to be who we really are. Toil saps us of our life and energy—the works of freedom actually help to regenerate our souls. That is why the Lord said in Matthew 11:28-30:

> **"Come to Me, all who are weary and heavy-laden, and I will give you rest.**

"Take My yoke upon you, and learn from Me, for I am gentle and humble in heart; and you shall find rest for your souls.

"For My yoke is easy, and My load is light."

A yoke is for work, but when we are yoked with the Lord and His purposes, which is what we were created for, we actually find rest and refreshment for our souls instead of weariness. The work may actually be harder when we are laboring for the Lord than it was when we labored for "Pharaoh and his taskmasters," but it will be far more fulfilling.

This is why many people have a basic goal of going into business for themselves instead of working for someone else. This is a step in the right direction, but it is not necessarily the same as working for the King. Even more than being created for labor, man was created to have a special relationship with God, which is even more fundamental to who we are than what we do. Without that relationship, we will still be empty, regardless of how successful we are otherwise.

The greatest reward that we can ever have, more than any treasure or possessions we could gain on this earth, will be to hear on that great judgment day, **"Well done, good and faithful servant!" (see Matthew 25:21 NIV)** The greatest reward we can ever know is to bring pleasure to the Lord.

Now we do not have to wait until the judgment day to know the approval of the Lord. Neither do we have to go into traditional ministry or a "Christian business" to work for the King and His kingdom. In fact, you can start today regardless of what job you have. As Paul wrote in Colossians 3:23-24,

Whatever you do, do your work heartily, as for the Lord rather than for men;

knowing that from the Lord you will receive the reward of the inheritance. It is the Lord Christ whom you serve.

It does not matter how boring your present job seems, you can turn it into worship, and if you do your work for the Lord, rather than just for the company or your employer, you will begin to experience the greatest freedom and satisfaction in your work that you can imagine. This will happen even though the work itself may not change. It is better to be a slave and have the presence of the Lord than to be a king without Him. If you experience this, you will be a free person, regardless of what job or position you are in. If you do not know this truth, you will never be a free person, regardless of what job or position you are in.

The freedom of the kingdom is in the heart, not our circumstances. If we will become free in our hearts, then it will usually carry over into our circumstances. Even if it does not change the circumstances, we can have a feast right in the presence of our enemies.

I have experienced working for myself by owning my own business. It can be very satisfying. However, in many ways, there can be a major bondage that comes with it, such as not being able to just leave the job at 5 o'clock, on weekends, or anytime for that matter. It was not long before I started to envy the people who worked for me, because when they were off work, they were really free. I was not. I may have made more money, but time is more valuable than money, and I lost the ability to have my own time.

Progressive Liberty

There is a principle about bondage that we must also understand so we can use our freedom rightly. Those who have been in prison have often said that after their release it was almost impossible for them to make even the simplest decisions. In prison, a person's "decision maker" will atrophy, and it can take years to rebuild it so that one can take authority and responsibility again. In prison, every decision is made for the inmates and when they get out, even a simple decision can be daunting. This is the reason why many who get out of prison actually want to return after being out for just a little while. Some will even commit crimes hoping to be caught. To these, the greatest freedom was *to not* have any freedom, and therefore to not have to make decisions.

This is why the Israelites got out of Egypt in one night, but it took forty years to get the Egypt out of them. After just a few difficulties, they even desired to go back to bondage in Egypt, rather than continue their quest toward freedom. It is the same for Christians who are set free from bondage to sin, but are terrified by their freedom, and often fail purposely when they are told that they have to choose not to sin.

Mankind was created to be free, and there is no question that this is the best state to be in, and the only one in which we will ever become what we were created to be. However, there is a good reason why Paul wrote for slaves to not be worried about being a slave, but rather to consider themselves the Lord's freedmen. He also said that those who were free were the Lord's slaves. He went on to say that if a slave had the opportunity to become free, and wanted to, they should do this, but they could be free without doing it (see I Corinthians 7:21-22). Freedom is hard, and it requires a maturity to be able to handle it that not many yet have.

The present employee-to-owner relationship can be a form of slavery. There were slave owners who cared for their slaves, and those who mistreated them, just as there are employers who care for their people, and those who mistreat them. Even so, without question, the employee serves the employer. However, if we are employees, we should take Paul's exhortation that if we are called while a slave or employee, we should not worry about it because we can be just as free in the Spirit. If you really do not want to be someone else's employee, it is not a sin, and you can become free of this relationship, but it may not make you free. The truly free have liberty in any circumstance, in any job, and even in slavery or prison.

With freedom comes responsibility. If you are free to make decisions, you are also responsible for the consequences of your decisions. When I was free not to have an employer, but became the employer of others, suddenly I was not just looking out for my own family, but for those of all of my employees as well. Soon I was in the place where my decisions could affect many people. This was, by far, a heavier yoke than I had ever known before.

The freedom to make decisions is not without cost, but can be the heaviest yoke of all. This is almost impossible to see or understand until you experience it. I have watched many people who were constantly critical of their boss, pastor, or even their government completely change their views when they were promoted to a similar responsibility.

As we are warned in Galatians 6:7, **"Do not be deceived, God is not mocked; for whatever a man sows, this he will also reap."** If you have been critical and rebellious as an employee or as a church member toward the leadership of your church, you can count on having to face the same as an employer or church leader. The things that you thought and may have been totally convinced of when you were an employee or church member, you will almost certainly see differently when you are in the position of leadership. Just as no child can really understand what it is like to be a parent until he or she is one, this may seem impossible to you now, but it is true.

Right now we all have the freedom to choose our own attitudes, and it is definitely in our best interest to choose a good one. "**...Do not turn your freedom into an opportunity for the flesh, but through love serve one another**" **(see Galatians 5:13).** We are even commanded to love our enemies, because unless we love them, we will not be able to judge them rightly. In fact, we will not judge anything properly without love, as we are told in Philippians 1:9-11:

> **And this I pray, that your love may abound still more and more in real knowledge and all discernment,**
>
> **so that you may approve the things that are excellent, in order to be sincere and blameless until the day of Christ;**
>
> **having been filled with the fruit of righteousness which comes through Jesus Christ, to the glory and praise of God.**

We see here that "**real knowledge and all discernment**" are the result of love abounding. This is also how we will be able to "**approve the things that are excellent,**" be "**blameless until the day of Christ,**" and be "**filled with the fruit of righteousness.**" True freedom, which is what we have been called into and is our condition in the kingdom, is for the purpose of loving God and loving others. Love is the greatest freedom. Selfishness is the greatest bondage.

True love is always proactive. True love serves. You can do that right now regardless of the job or position you are in. If you start now and remain faithful, you will bear fruit, and you will be trusted with more freedom, because you will be ever more responsible.

True love **"does not seek its own,"** (see I Corinthians 13:5) so we are not seeking love in order to just be our own boss, but in order to carry even more of the burdens of the people—to serve them. If we are doing it this way, we are being yoked with Christ and the burdens will not be heavy. We will actually be exhilarated by them. This is a worthy goal—to be more free so that we can carry more responsibility and bear more fruit for the sake of the Lord and His people.

God's people are called to be "kings and priests" with Christ. There is no greater honor that we could ever have. The rest of the creation marvels at this opportunity given to mankind. It is a worthy quest to want to grow in authority when it is based on love for our King, serving His interests and serving His people. True authority in Christ is actually to be a slave of Christ, and being a slave of His is the most free we can ever be.

Be Filled First

One reason why we spent so much time examining the works of the flesh before doing this study is because our carnal, selfish nature must be dealt with before we will be entrusted with the true riches of the kingdom. Some of this is dealt with as we learn to handle earthly riches. Even so, we are not just trying to stop manifesting the works of the flesh, but we are seeking to bear fruit for the kingdom. If we just pursue the negative, we will only become empty. If we pursue the positive, it will displace the negative. Then we will be full of the Lord rather than just empty of ourselves.

I have heard many Christians say that they are seeking to decrease so that Christ may increase in them. That may seem to be an honorable devotion, but it is not a very wise one. They think they are just pursuing what John the Baptist pursued, but that is, in fact, the opposite of what he said, which was **"He must increase, but I must decrease" (John 3:30)**. It is important that we not get this backwards. If Christ increases in your life, you will decrease. If you just try to decrease, you will get nothing but empty.

So our pursuit is not to just empty ourselves, but to be filled. True freedom will not come by just seeing how evil or bad we are, though that is a necessary step to bring about repentance. We must learn to crucify the flesh when it rises up and tries to assert itself. However, our goal is to behold the glory of the Lord and be changed into His image. This is ultimately a positive pursuit, not just a negative one, though we begin by becoming aware of how badly we need this change.

In this same way, we will not become free by just trying to be rid of our bondage. We are not just leaving our bondage, but we are pursuing liberty. One is a negative reaction, the other is a positive pursuit.

To be truly free, we need to even turn our bondage into a positive experience, being thankful for it and all that it taught us. In this I am not implying that we be thankful for the sin, but rather that we become thankful for every negative thing in our lives because it helped to lead us to Christ. In the end, if we are going to be truly free, there must be no negatives in our lives, but everything must be transformed into a glorious victory. Those who wounded us must be forgiven, and the bad things that happened to us must be seen as positive in the light of Romans 8:28, **"And we know that God causes all things to work together for good to those who love God, to those who are called according to His purpose."**

Again, it only took one night to get Israel out of Egypt, but it took a long process to get the Egypt out of them. True freedom never comes by just reacting to something, but it is a positive devotion to the kingdom of heaven. The only true freedom comes from the pursuit of Christ and doing His will. As much of a paradox as it seems at first, there is no greater freedom we could ever know than to be Christ's slave, thinking always about doing His will.

First, this will be our greatest freedom because the Lord is the ultimate benevolent King. He cares even more about our welfare than we do. He is also the ultimate wise King, who knows what is good for us far better than we do. He also made us, and therefore knows better than we ever could what we were made for. Therefore, the more devoted we are to doing His will every day, the more truly free we will be—free to be who we truly are.

Many think of freedom as the ability to do whatever they have a whim to do. That kind of "freedom" always leads to bondage of the worst kind. For example, if a train was freed from the tracks that restrained it so it could "be free" to just go charging across the countryside any place that it wanted, how far would it get? The track that restrains it is the very instrument of its true freedom—the freedom to do what it was created to do. Likewise, the restraints that the Lord has put on mankind are not just to hinder us from doing things that we want to do, but to keep us from doing the things that will hurt us and lead to our ultimate bondage—death. His restraints set us free to be all that we were created for.

The ultimate purpose that we were created for was to love the Lord. The second highest purpose that we were created for was to love one another. Therefore, the ultimate freedom that we can know is to love the Lord and love people. This is the greatest freedom because true love is freedom from ourselves and freedom from the ultimate bondage: self-centeredness.

How free would you be to do something if you knew that you absolutely could not fail at it? Then consider this: **"love never fails" (see I Corinthians 13:8)**. If we live our lives to love God and each other, we will never fail. What could be a greater freedom than this?

This is why all of the negatives of the Law were replaced by the Lord summing up the whole Law in the two positives—loving the Lord and loving each other. These fulfill the Law, because if we love God, we are not going to worship idols. If we love one another we will not murder, envy, steal, etc. If we do these two positives, we will fulfill the whole Law.

Therefore, we must not think in terms of these being duties we have to comply with, but that they are the wonderful things we get to do! We get to go to church and worship the Lord! We get to pray! We get to read our Bibles! If we see these things as just requirements or duties, we do not yet love. What person cannot wait for his conversation to be about the one he is passionately in love with? Who wants to stop being with or learning about the one they are truly in love with?

If our pursuit of the Lord, or righteousness, is on the basis of duties and obligations, we are still trapped in a religion, and we are not in the true faith. Duties and obligations are the foundation of religion. True Christianity is not just a religion, but a relationship with God. There is nothing more exciting, wonderful, or interesting than God. If we are walking with Him as we should, there will be a continual excitement and awe at this wonderful pursuit that we have. It will never be something we have to do, but something that we get to do, and it will be the major joy of our lives.

CHAPTER SEVENTEEN

THE GOOD SOIL

We will soon study the fruit of the Spirit, but first we are trying to prepare the ground for the seed so that it can bear fruit. The good soil for that seed is the church. Church life, with all of its blessings and problems, is required to bear the true fruit of the Spirit. The Scriptures are very clear about this, some of which we will view so that we can have a vision for this most important element of the true Christian life.

For those of you who already have a healthy church life, seek to excel even more and rise to even higher ground in all that you do. Determine that your church will be like the great churches of the New Testament which became famous for their love, faith, generosity, the missionaries that they sent out, and any other exploits that extended the kingdom. Determine that your church will be a great light set on a hill for as many as possible to see.

If you have drifted from church or do not have a healthy church life, it is my earnest prayer that this will change for you, and soon. In the time to come, being in your right place in the body of Christ will literally be essential for your survival. If you have for any reason become offended by the church, I pray that you will be convicted and challenged to repent of any unforgiveness (and there is some), and be inspired to return to the fold. Again, this can literally be a life or death decision. Never, ever give up on the church, just as the Lord has not given up on any of us.

Regardless of the church's failings and mistakes in the past, she has a most glorious destiny and will finish in victory. So can you. But if you are waiting for the church to get its act together before you give her another chance, she will soon be too far ahead for you to ever catch up.

Burnt Stones

The rebuilt temple, the one that was promised to have an even greater glory than the former one, was rebuilt out of "burnt stones" from the previous temple. If you have not been burned, or if you have not been disillusioned (which is to get rid of our illusions), you are not qualified for the greater house. Do not let your wounds from church life or your disappointments with the church hinder your future. They can be used to qualify you for a greater glory. Of course, for this to happen, previous experiences must be changed from bitterness into glory.

Just think about how disappointed the Lord should be with us, but He has not given up on us. We must not give up on Him or His ability to make His people into what they are called to be. The church on the earth is going to have a most glorious conclusion, and the Lord wants us to be a part of it. However, to do this we must give others the same kind of grace that we ourselves have received.

We know by the Scriptures that it is going to take faith and patience to inherit the promises. Have you ever wondered why we have this huge "faith movement," but no "patience movement?" It will take both faith and patience for us to inherit our Promised Land. If we want to grow in faith, we will have to be willing to be put in situations that will take more faith than we now have. If we want to grow in patience, we have to be willing to be put in situations that require more patience than we now have.

It may take more faith and patience to be in the church than just trying to walk with God alone, but this is an opportunity for us to grow. We must believe for the church to become all that the prophecies of Scripture say that it will be, regardless of past experiences. Are we going to elevate our past experiences above the Word of God? Don't miss your calling and destiny! Get vitally involved in a local church!

If you answer that there just is not a good church close by, then join a bad one. That may be the greatest opportunity of all to grow up into the nature of Christ. He joined mankind when we did not look like much. If you cannot find a church with people you like, or whom you agree with, that may be even better than finding one that you feel comfortable in now. Just remember, you are going to be a trial to them just as they may be to you, but these trials are an opportunity for all to be changed into His image if we will love each other.

I had a friend who used to work hard to get his pH levels perfect in his swimming pool. Then he realized that if he got them perfect, just as soon as he jumped into the pool they would be out of whack again. Many people likewise want the church to be perfect before they jump in, but if that were the case, as soon as they jumped in, it would be messed up again. The ones who will be a part of the perfect church will be those who go through the process with everyone else. Unless you are now perfect, you are much better off to find an imperfect congregation to join!

If you answer that there just is not a church, good or bad, close by, then either get used to driving long distances to the meetings or move. If we really are seeking the kingdom first, which we must do if we expect to receive the promise of having everything else added to us, we will choose where we live by kingdom purposes first.

The church is not the whole kingdom of God, but it is the foundation of the kingdom of God. Church life is the foundation of all kingdom life. At this time, building His church is the main thing He is doing on the earth, and the church will be used to prepare the way for and usher in His kingdom. Move to the place where you can be vitally involved in this great work of the kingdom, not just to a place where you can get a better job. If we are seeking His kingdom first, we will move to be in the church we are supposed to be in, and trust that everything else, including our jobs, will work out, just as He promises. This will take faith, but faith is what we are called to walk in, and without it we cannot please Him.

Run to the Light

There can be times when we are called to draw aside and seek the Lord, and we may forego fellowship for a time to do this. However, if this is what we are called to do, we will not be running from a negative situation in the church to do it. We are called to go from glory to glory, victory to victory, not defeat to defeat. We should never leave a situation without getting the victory in it. If we are called to a time of solitude before the Lord, it will most likely come when we are enjoying the fellowship of the saints too much.

I have learned the hard way not to trust any Christian who does not have a vital local church life. In every case to date that I have compromised and trusted someone who was not vitally involved in a local church, there has surfaced in that person a major problem, and they created major problems for me and our ministry.

Satan dwells in darkness, which is his domain. His power comes by keeping us in his domain. If we have a truly healthy church life, the relationships will become so close that we will not be able to hide who we really are very well. I do believe that most who refrain from a vital local church life are hiding something. They may not even know it themselves, because deception is deceptive, but there is something in them that does not want to be exposed to the light. If for no other reason than dwelling in the light and not being able to hide who we are, we need a vital, real, local church life. If you do not have one, get one, fast. There is probably nothing more important that you can do in your life at this time.

If the above exhortation has offended you, then you are the one I am talking about who has strongholds in your life that are exalting themselves above the purposes of God. If I have offended you with this, then something is trying to keep you in darkness. Be honest with yourself and God, and repent. It is simply not possible to be properly joined to the Head without being properly joined to His body as well.

The time is now upon us when no one will make it who is not a vital member of the body of Christ. No minister will make it long who is not a vital member of a team, which true New Testament ministry is. True Christianity is not a religion as much as it is a relationship with God and His people. The health of our faith is dependent on each of these, which is why we are told in I John 1:6-8:

If we say that we have fellowship with Him and yet walk in the darkness, we lie and do not practice the truth;

> but if we walk in the light as He Himself is in the light, we have fellowship with one another, and the blood of Jesus His Son cleanses us from all sin.
>
> If we say that we have no sin, we are deceiving ourselves, and the truth is not in us.

Many claim to have such a special fellowship with the Lord that they can forego fellowship with His people. According to the clear Word of God, this is not possible. If we have a special fellowship with God, we will be one with His people in the church also. The Greek word that is translated **"fellowship"** in the text above is *koinonia,* which is also sometimes translated "communion." This is much more than a handshake or slap on the back when we see each other at a church service—it is a vital, intertwined relationship that makes two or more people inseparable.

If a part of our body was to be severed, it could not live very long without being quickly and properly reattached. The same is true with any member of the Lord's body. It is by having this *koinonia* fellowship that **"the blood of Jesus His Son cleanses us from all sin."** Just as the parts of our body have to be properly joined to each other for the blood to flow through them, the same is true of His body, the church. Because **"the life of the flesh is in the blood" (see Leviticus 17:11),** this metaphor implies that His life will flow through the church that is properly joined together, which is also what we are told in Ephesians 4:11-16:

> And He gave some as apostles, and some as prophets, and some as evangelists, and some as pastors and teachers,
>
> for the equipping of the saints for the work of service, to the building up of the body of Christ;
>
> until we all attain to the unity of the faith, and of the knowledge of the Son of God, to a mature man, to the measure of the stature which belongs to the fulness of Christ.
>
> As a result, we are no longer to be children, tossed here and there by waves, and carried about by every wind of doctrine, by the trickery of men, by craftiness in deceitful scheming;
>
> but speaking the truth in love, we are to grow up in all aspects into Him, who is the head, even Christ,
>
> from whom the whole body, being fitted and held together by that which every joint supplies, according to the proper working of each individual part, causes the growth of the body for the building up of itself in love.

First, this exhortation is not until *some* of us attain, but **"until we all attain" (verse 13)**. When we attain, it is obvious that the whole body will be properly fit together with each part "properly working," which causes the growth and the building in love. We must understand that we are not going to get to where we are called to be without the rest of the body. Therefore, regardless of your previous experience in the church, start loving the church. It is His body. It is composed of His own children. Regardless of their present condition, we should love them for His sake. As it is made clear in I John 4:19-21:

We love, because He first loved us.

If someone says, "I love God," and hates his brother, he is a liar; for the one who does not love his brother whom he has seen, cannot love God whom he has not seen.

And this commandment we have from Him, that the one who loves God should love his brother also.

If we truly love Him, we must also love His people. We are members of one another, and if one part of your body gets severely injured, or becomes infected, the whole body can suffer. We, too, are composed the same way in the Spirit. Therefore, it behooves us to love and minister to each other even if for no other reason than we need each other to make it. Need sometimes precedes love, but let our goal be to love.

Just as Israel crossed over into the Promised Land as separate tribes, but one nation, the Lord's body is also composed of many different movements, or denominations, but we are one body in Him. All of the tribes were commanded to fight for their fellow tribes until all had entered into their inheritance. We, too, must do the same.

Therefore, we should rejoice when any church or movement makes advances, takes new ground, or has any kind of breakthrough. When anyone does, it is truly for the sake of us all. Just as the different tribes helped each other possess their inheritance and could not go back to their own inheritance until all had attained theirs, we need to be willing to join others while they are fighting for their inheritance. Even though it is not our inheritance specifically, it is ours in the sense that we are all members of one another.

It is for this reason that I began years ago to make a habit of praying for every church I pass, every ministry I see on television, and anytime I hear of great things going on in another church or ministry, praying for them to excel even more. If a congregation close to us begins to have problems that we are made aware of, we try to help. We must start seeing our inheritance as being linked to the fortunes of the whole body of Christ.

The high priest had a breastplate on which he carried a stone for each tribe of Israel. This was so that all of God's people would be carried on his heart. If we are going to walk in the high calling, we, too, must carry all of God's people on our hearts. The ultimate fruit of the Promised Land is love. When Christians start to love each other, the church will become the most glorious place on earth. It will then be a land that all marvel at and desire to be a part of.

To understand the Promised Land of God, we must understand the fruit of the Spirit. We have been tilling the ground in the last couple of chapters so that we can cultivate this fruit. I realize that most of you are already walking in much of this or you would not be reading a book such as this, but now let us seek to excel more and more.

There may be some new insights into the fruit of the Spirit in these coming studies, but that is not my point in writing this. Sometimes, we just need to have the seeds that have already been planted in us watered so that they can grow. Whether we are planting new insights, or just watering old ones, the point is to grow in the fruit of the Spirit. Then, with the foundation of a right character, we can be trusted with more power and authority until the Promised Land is not only conquered, but possessed as an inheritance.

CHAPTER EIGHTEEN

SEIZE THE DAY

We have been briefly discussing how the seedbed of the fruit of the Spirit is New Testament church life. Of course, another main seedbed of this fruit is family life. This is why both of these, church life and family life, are under such an assault in our time. However, it is during these times that the greatest church life, and the greatest families, will emerge.

As we considered earlier, the Lord Jesus could have bound the devil and taken possession of the world immediately after His resurrection, as He had fully purchased it through the cross. However, before taking possession of this world He wanted to give an opportunity for many others to become sons and daughters of the King. Their faithfulness would be proven by enduring the onslaught of the world and the devil.

Since the Fall, the devil has had a boast. His boast is that the Lord's crowning creation, mankind, which He created especially to have fellowship and dwell with, when given the choice, chose evil over righteousness, even when living in the most perfect conditions.

Because of this, the devil boasts that given the choice all of creation will choose his ways over the Lord's ways. However, before the end of this age comes, the Lord will have a people who will have ended this boast. Even in the darkest of times, in the worst conditions, against the onslaught of all that hell and the world can throw at them, they will remain faithful, choose righteousness over evil, and obey God rather than the evil one. In this way they will even become witnesses to principalities and powers, as well as the rest of creation that God and His truth will always ultimately triumph.

Therefore, the greater the trial, the greater the witness. Even the angels will admit that the church, which has endured the greatest of trials and remained faithful, is worthy to be their judges. For this reason the greatest fruit of the Spirit is grown in the most difficult conditions, which is why we are given the important exhortation in James 1:2-4, 12:

> **Consider it all joy, my brethren, when you encounter various trials,**
>
> **knowing that the testing of your faith produces endurance.**
>
> **And let endurance have its perfect result, that you may be perfect and complete, lacking in nothing.**
>
> **Blessed is a man who perseveres under trial; for once he has been approved, he will**

receive the crown of life, which the Lord has promised to those who love Him.

Just as runners' endurance does not increase until they press past their previous limits, our faith does not grow until we are placed in conditions that require more faith than we have had before. Our love does not grow until we are placed in a situation where it requires more than we have had before. The same is true of our patience, our peace, and so on. For this reason, as long as we remain on the path of life, we can expect to go through some trials that are helping us to grow. When we learn this, these trials do not become things to be avoided, but embraced as opportunities, and the joy that James talked about.

As Francis Frangipane has said, "We never fail one of God's tests—we just keep taking them until we pass." I think most of us are now ready to stop taking the same tests over and over, so let's pass them and move on. Then we shall receive the reward that God gives to all who pass His tests—even bigger ones!

This is true. The bigger the trial, the bigger the opportunity to enter into the kingdom. This truth strengthened saints in the first century, as we are told in Acts 14:22, "**...strengthening the souls of the disciples, encouraging them to continue in the faith, and saying, 'Through many tribulations we must enter the kingdom of God.'**" Only the weak, immature, or deceived fail to see trials as gateways into the kingdom and opportunities to grow in the fruit of the Spirit, which is to grow up into Christ.

Those who want to live lives of escape where they can avoid all trials are those who will fail to mature. The sad thing is that they will have trials anyway, and because of their failure to face them properly, they will be increasingly defeated by them instead of strengthened. These go from defeat to defeat, usually growing in self-pity instead of the nature of the Lord. Once we learn how overcoming a trial strengthens us in the Lord and how much sweeter victory tastes, learning to go from victory to victory, never leaving a situation in defeat, will cause us to see greater trials as the opportunity to taste even sweeter victories, leading us deeper into the kingdom.

God does not tempt men with evil, but we are told throughout the Scriptures that the Lord does test the righteous. There is a difference between a test and a temptation, though a temptation may be a test. The Lord tested Adam and Eve by placing the Tree of the Knowledge of Good and Evil in the Garden. This was not done to cause them to sin; however, there could have been no true obedience if there was no freedom to disobey. There can be no true worship if there is no freedom not to worship. It is for this reason that there must be freedom for there to be true worship. This freedom requires that we choose.

We must choose to believe. We most choose to love. We must choose to be patient. We must choose the fruit of the right tree. Adam and Eve could have complained that if the Lord did not want them to eat from the Tree of the Knowledge of Good and Evil, why did He put it right in the middle of the Garden, and why did He make it so appealing? Because it would not have been a test if it had not been appealing. And like that tree, most of our tests are placed right in the middle of our lives where it is very difficult not to face them.

We can make the same complaints, "Lord, why don't You just bind Satan now so that he can't tempt us? Why don't You just remove the temptations?" Then it would not be a test of our faith, our love, or our devotion, and we would not grow. We must understand that the harder the trial, the more the Lord thinks of us, not less. In fact, it should concern us greatly if we are not going through trials or are not being disciplined by the Lord. We are told this in one of the most important exhortations in Scripture, which I quote below and encourage you to read carefully. The written Word of God is the seed, the fertilizer, and the water required for us to bear the true fruit of the Spirit:

> **Therefore, since we have so great a cloud of witnesses surrounding us, let us also lay aside every encumbrance, and the sin which so easily entangles us, and let us run with endurance the race that is set before us,**

> **fixing our eyes on Jesus, the author and perfecter of faith, who for the joy set before Him endured the cross, despising the shame, and has sat down at the right hand of the throne of God.**

For consider Him who has endured such hostility by sinners against Himself, so that you may not grow weary and lose heart.

You have not yet resisted to the point of shedding blood in your striving against sin;

and you have forgotten the exhortation which is addressed to you as sons, "My son, do not regard lightly the discipline of the Lord, nor faint when you are reproved by Him;

For those whom the Lord loves He disciplines, and He scourges every son whom He receives."

It is for discipline that you endure; God deals with you as with sons; for what son is there whom his father does not discipline?

But if you are without discipline, of which all have become partakers, then you are illegitimate children and not sons.

Furthermore, we had earthly fathers to discipline us, and we respected them; shall we not much rather be subject to the Father of spirits, and live?

For they disciplined us for a short time as seemed best to them, but He disciplines us for our good, that we may share His holiness.

All discipline for the moment seems not to be joyful, but sorrowful; yet to those who have been trained by it, afterwards it yields the peaceful fruit of righteousness.

Therefore, strengthen the hands that are weak and the knees that are feeble,

and make straight paths for your feet, so that the limb which is lame may not be put out of joint, but rather be healed (Hebrews 12:1-13).

If we are going to bear fruit, we cannot keep wasting our trials, but must steel our resolve to believe God, and trust in the sure fact that He "**...always leads us in His triumph in Christ, and manifests through us the sweet aroma of the knowledge of Him in every place" (II Corinthians 2:14).** We are also encouraged by His sure Word that "**...we know that God causes all things to work together for good to those who love God, to those who are called according to His purpose. For whom He foreknew, He also predestined to become conformed to the image of His Son, that He might be the first-born among many brethren; and whom He predestined, these He also called; and whom He called, these He also justified; and whom He justified, these He also glorified" (Romans 8:28-30).**

This is the sure Word of God that will never fail! We can only fail if we quit living according to His

Word. Just as the first thing the devil did to cause Adam and Eve to stumble was to get them to doubt God's Word. We must, above all things, resolve to hold fast to His Word, knowing that it is true.

All of God's tests are open book tests where the answers are readily available to us. However, just knowing the answers is not enough—we must live them. The real test of whether we believe the Lord is whether we live according to His Word. Determine today and every day that you will not run from the tests, but resolve to recognize them and pass them. In the following chapters, we will go into more detail about just how we can more readily recognize and understand these tests and use each of them to grow in the fruit of the Spirit.

CHAPTER NINETEEN

ONE HEART WITH THE KING

As we continue our study on the fruit of the kingdom, we will begin with the most important text in the Bible about bearing fruit, which is the statement of the Lord Himself on this matter, as recorded in John 15:1-8:

"I am the true vine, and My Father is the vinedresser.

"Every branch in Me that does not bear fruit, He takes away; and every branch that bears fruit, He prunes it, that it may bear more fruit.

"You are already clean because of the word which I have spoken to you.

"Abide in Me, and I in you. As the branch cannot bear fruit of itself, unless it abides in the vine, so neither can you, unless you abide in Me.

"I am the vine, you are the branches; he who abides in Me, and I in him, he bears much fruit; for apart from Me you can do nothing.

"If anyone does not abide in Me, he is thrown away as a branch, and dries up; and they gather them, and cast them into the fire, and they are burned.

"If you abide in Me, and My words abide in you, ask whatever you wish, and it shall be done for you.

"By this is My Father glorified, that you bear much fruit, and so prove to be My disciples."

By this we can deduct several important facts:

1) We can only bear fruit if we abide in the Lord; apart from Him we can do nothing.

2) If we are abiding in Him, we will bear fruit. If we are not bearing fruit, it is evidence that we are not truly abiding in Him.

3) When we do begin to bear fruit, we can expect to be pruned so that we can bear even more fruit.

4) It is by bearing **"much fruit"** that we glorify the Father and prove to be His disciples.

5) If we do not bear fruit, we will be cut off.

6) If we abide in Him, we can ask whatever we wish and it will be done for us.

To be a Christian, growing in the fruit of the Spirit and bearing fruit for the kingdom is not an option. It is so essential that it proves whether we are true disciples or not. If we are not bearing fruit, we can expect to be cut off from the Vine. It is that important. However, He did not call us to cut us off, but to help us to abide in Him so that we can live the most fruitful, purposeful lives that we could ever live on this earth. That is your calling, and what you can even now live in, regardless of any earthly circumstances, including age, present health, or any other conditions. If you have a single day left on the earth you can, in fact, be used to do something historic for the kingdom if you will abide in Him today.

Before going any further, we need to understand that the concept of salvation being based on the mere belief that God exists is an affront to the God who exists, and it is not only intellectual foolishness, but is in basic conflict with the Scriptures. The demons believe that He exists. The demons believe in Jesus, and even in the atonement of the cross. In fact, they do not have nearly the doubts about these things that many Christians do. The belief that results in salvation is not simply the belief in the existence of these things; it is putting our trust in them. The Word of God is also clear that those with true faith in God will live for Him.

Those who really believe in Him will be devoted to knowing Him—knowing what pleases Him and what He expects of us, so that we can do what He says. For true discipleship there are no other options. Consider the following statements that the Lord Jesus Himself made in Matthew 16:24-26:

Then Jesus said to His disciples, "If anyone wishes to come after Me, let him deny himself, and take up his cross, and follow Me.

"For whoever wishes to save his life shall lose it; but whoever loses his life for My sake shall find it.

"For what will a man be profited, if he gains the whole world, and forfeits his soul? Or what will a man give in exchange for his soul?"

Anyone who is more focused on this life and in producing for this life than for eternity, obviously does not understand true discipleship. How could anyone who truly grasps the truth of the gospel not do all things for the sake of the gospel? This does not mean that we cannot have and be successful in secular professions, but even in those we are doing all that we do as unto the Lord and not just for ourselves. True disciples do not live for themselves, but for Him. The truly redeemed no longer belong to themselves; they were bought with a price and now belong to the One who purchased them.

"So therefore, no one of you can be My disciple who does not give up all his own possessions.

"Therefore, salt is good; but if even salt has become tasteless, with what will it be seasoned?

"It is useless either for the soil or for the manure pile; it is thrown out. He who has ears to hear, let him hear" (Luke 14:33-35).

Many draw back from this text just as the rich young ruler did. This does not necessarily mean that we need to go out right away and give everything we own to the Lord. What it does mean is that we do not consider anything that we have in our possession as our possession, but something we have been made a steward over.

A good steward does not just freely spend or make decisions about anything which belongs to his master, but earnestly seeks the will of his master about such matters. Having this mentality about our possessions will help us to abide in the Lord.

"And why do you call Me, 'Lord, Lord,' and do not do what I say?

"Everyone who comes to Me, and hears My words, and acts upon them, I will show you whom he is like:

he is like a man building a house, who dug deep and laid a foundation upon the rock; and when a flood rose, the torrent burst against that house and could not shake it, because it had been well built.

"But the one who has heard, and has not acted accordingly, is like a man who built a house upon the ground without any foundation; and the torrent burst against it

and immediately it collapsed, and the ruin of that house was great" (Luke 6:46-49).

To hear the Words of the Lord are not enough, and may in fact have us feeling safe in a condition in which we are still in eternal jeopardy. If He is our Lord, the One whose authority we submit to, we will do what He commands. We can go to church services every time the doors open, but if we are not living according to His Words, it will not profit us. True discipleship is demonstrated by devoted obedience to His Words, not just hearing them. Spurgeon once lamented that he could find ten men who would die for the Bible for every one who would read it!

How can we abide in His Words if we do not know them? Can we be true disciples of His when we spend more time reading the sports page, news, or books, listening to tapes and resources other than the Bible? This is not saying that we cannot have an interest in these things, but if that interest in these temporary things eclipses our interest in eternal things, have they not become idols that we love more than God and His purposes?

If Jesus, who was the Word Himself, took His stand on the written Word when challenged by the devil, how much more should we know the written Word and take our stand in life on it? Without question, true disciples are devoted to knowing the written Word of God, and they are devoted to obeying it.

"If you abide in My word, then you are truly disciples of Mine;

and you shall know the truth, and the truth shall make you free" (John 8:31-32).

The Scriptures are clear about the definition of a true disciple and true freedom. True freedom comes by living above the cares and worries of this world and from not being bound by sin. This does not mean we are not responsible for the things of this world that we are made stewards of. In fact, we can be trusted with far more responsibility because of the solid foundation of faith in the Lord that we have. To live by faith in the Lord, instead of in the conditions of this world, is to live in a kingdom that simply cannot be shaken, regardless of what happens in this world. That is true freedom indeed.

"By this all men will know that you are My disciples, if you have love for one another" (John 13:35).

The Scriptures are also very clear about what love is, and we will look at it in some depth in this study. Without love all of our works become vain, as we are told in I Corinthians 13:2-3, **"And if I have the gift of prophecy, and know all mysteries and all knowledge; and if I have all faith, so as to remove mountains, but do not have love, I am nothing. And if I give all my possessions to feed the poor, and if I deliver my body to be burned, but do not have love, it profits me nothing."** Therefore, the pursuit of love is something we definitely want to give the highest priority. Think about it. What percentage of our lives do we devote to growing in love?

"By this is My Father glorified, that you bear much fruit, and so prove to be My disciples" (John 15:8).

As we have already addressed at the beginning of this study, one of the ways it is proven that we are true disciples is not just by bearing some fruit, but **"much fruit."** Should this not be a priority in our lives? Can we look back at our lives and see **"much fruit"**? Do we see the potential for it in the future? There are very practical ways that we can be assured that we do, which is the purpose of this study. We want to take the time to examine them with the devotion of doing them. What is taking our time, attention, and resources that is more important than this?

The way that we will do this is not by just focusing on the fruit itself, but the One in whom we must abide in order to bear fruit. Apart from Him, we can do nothing and in Him we can do anything. That is the contrast between our choices. If we are abiding in Him, as He promises, we can ask whatever we wish and it will be done for us. Of course, if we are abiding in Him, we would only ask that which is His will anyway. Even so, our choice is between doing nothing, or anything that we wish, to bring glory to His name.

This means that any Christian could be used to do even the greatest exploits. There are no limits on anyone who abides in Him. A new believer who learns to better abide in the Lord can accomplish far more for the kingdom than the most knowledgeable seminary professor, the most seemingly successful pastor, the most popular teacher, or an author who writes many books. The goal is not just to do work, but to do His work, with Him.

This is not to detract from the noble purposes of teaching, being a pastor, or writing, if that is what we are called to do, but simply learning to abide in Him is more important. For this, you do not have to go to seminary, you do not have to go to college, and you do not have to have a high I.Q. It is far more important to have a devotion to know the Lord and to do His will. You may not be able to even lead a home group, but if you learn to abide in the Lord, you could be the one to save a city or even a nation. You could be the one who ignites the greatest revival in history; or you could be the one who walks on water, raises the dead, or moves mountains by your faith. There are no limits on anyone who abides in the Lord.

Without question, the greatest success we can have in this life will depend on how well we have abided in the Lord. No other factor in our lives, including our education, where we were born, who we know, or the material wealth we have, will be even close to having the influence on the true success of our lives as this one factor.

Nothing in human history ever so leveled the playing field for true success as the Lord Himself did for all who respond to the call to be His disciples. Any Christian on earth, regardless of all other circumstances, could become the greatest champion of the faith in the last days. Any Christian has the opportunity to become the Lord's best friend on the earth. What could we possibly have better to do with our lives?

CHAPTER TWENTY

THE FRUIT OF THE TREE OF LIFE

The fruit of the Spirit is listed in Galatians 5:22-23:

But the fruit of the Spirit is love, joy, peace, patience, kindness, goodness, faithfulness, gentleness, self-control....

These are the characteristics which all Christians should manifest in their lives, and will if they are true disciples. This does not mean that a disciple will be perfect all of the time, but true Christian discipleship, which is a life devoted to following Christ, learning His ways, and being changed into His image, will cause a person to grow in these things because they are the nature of Christ.

The metaphor for these characteristics is called **"fruit"** for a reason. These are not things that we can just begin to understand and then possess, but they must be grown and cultivated. Cultivation requires the preparation of the soil, planting, watering, weeding, protection from parasites, trimming, and pruning; then harvesting at the proper time. This is the kind of devotion that it requires to grow in the fruit of the Spirit.

If we do nothing to a field, we cannot expect anything more than just sporadic fruit to grow, at best, and it is far more likely to yield nothing but weeds and useless shrubs. To grow fruit takes much planning and careful work. The same is true with the fruit of the Spirit. In Psalm 37:3-6 we are told to:

> **Trust in the Lord, and do good; dwell in the land and cultivate faithfulness.**

> **Delight yourself in the Lord, and He will give you the desires of your heart.**

> **Commit your way to the Lord, trust also in Him, and He will do it.**

> **And He will bring forth your righteousness as the light, and your judgment as the noonday.**

Lilo Keller, a friend from Switzerland, once shared an interesting observation at one of our roundtables. She remarked how the gypsies were some of the most wonderful, interesting, and gifted people, but there was not one single case in history of a gypsy making a significant contribution to art, science, or culture. They never settled down in one place so as to sink roots deep enough to bear significant fruit. The same is true of many Christians. They can be extremely gifted, but they drift about so much that their roots are never able to go deep enough to bear significant fruit.

This is why a committed local church life and devotion to family are so crucial to bearing fruit. If we do not take the time to really work a field and cultivate it, we will not reap anything more than the occasional fruit we happen upon that grows wild. We may occasionally show love, peace, or patience, but it will be more sporadic than who we really are. The Lord wants to change our basic nature so we are love, joy, peace, and patience, and only rarely would we ever be anything but these things. We can only become this by the cultivation of the fruit, and giving ourselves to working on each one—planting seeds, watering them, and keeping the garden weeded.

Some may protest that this is not the **"fruit of the Spirit,"** but the result of human effort. With all that the Spirit accomplishes concerning man, He does through man. In everything there is a cooperation required.

When God created man, He put him in the Garden to cultivate it. This implies that the Garden was not complete without man's input. Of course, the Lord could do everything without us, but He has chosen not to. He wants a partnership in everything, from cultivating and keeping the original Garden of Eden, to cultivating and keeping the garden that is our own heart. He will lead us, guide us, and work with us, but the quality and amount of what is grown does depend a great deal on our faithfulness and devotion. We have responsibilities. We will make choices that will determine, to a great degree, what we become and the fruit we bear.

What we give our time and attention to is what is truly important to us. Those whose hearts are truly fixed on eternity will give themselves to that which will last forever. This is why the Lord said that He wants us to bear fruit that remains. The Apostle Paul also wrote in I Corinthians 3 about building that which would remain after the fire had tested it. As we read in Ephesians 1:10, the ultimate conclusion of all things is **"...the summing up of all things in Christ, things in the heavens and things upon the earth."** What will last longer than anything else in heaven or in earth is that which is of Christ. Therefore, if we are wise, we will be far more devoted to growing in His nature and doing His work than anything else in our lives.

As we discussed previously, there were four basic reasons why man was created:

1) To have fellowship with God.

2) To cultivate the Garden.

3) To be fruitful and multiply.

4) To rule over the earth.

These are still the four main purposes for which each one of us is here. To be fulfilled, which is to fulfill our purpose, means that we must become what we were created to be and do what we were created to do, which means that we will fulfill these primary purposes of man. If people are not growing in these, they will be frustrated and in discord to that degree.

We have each been given a spiritual garden just like the first man and woman. We must each discover our garden—the place that we have been given to cultivate, to bear fruit in, and to take spiritual dominion over. However, for this to work we must walk with God in our garden. The Lord intended for this to be a joint venture with Him.

The gardens that all of us have are our own hearts. As we are exhorted in Proverbs 4:23, **"Watch over your heart with all diligence, for from it flow the springs of life."** We must watch over the seeds that we allow to be sown in our own hearts. We need to be sure that the good seed is watered, and that the weeds, the cares and worries of this world, are rooted out. We need to watch over these seeds until the plant matures and there is fruit.

We also all have the gardens of our own families. We need to do the same thing here. If we do not cultivate righteousness and the fruit of the Spirit in our families, we should not be surprised when the works of the flesh start to manifest instead of the fruit we hoped for.

We also need to consider the places where we worship, work, and shop, and the neighborhoods that we live in, to be gardens that the Lord has given us to cultivate fruit in. We need to be sowing seeds, watering them, and taking spiritual authority over all of these places until we have fruit. We must remember that we are here to bear fruit, and if we are abiding in the Vine, we will, wherever we are planted.

Cultivation means work and it means responsibility. If we are cultivating these gardens where we are, we will not be so prone to pack up and leave them for a better job opportunity. Many Christians are not in the geographical will of God for their lives because they have chosen where they live by a job opportunity rather than by seeking the kingdom first. If we seek the kingdom first, He promises that everything else, which should include the jobs we need, will be taken care of.

There will be no true peace or true fulfillment in anything we accomplish on this earth, if it is not the result of our seeking first His kingdom. If we are not doing this, we will not be abiding in the Vine and we will, therefore, not be bearing the fruit that will really count when all things are counted on that great Judgment Day.

Those who truly love the Lord above all things will always seek His kingdom and His purposes first. Those who do not are serving idols that they have allowed to eclipse Him in their devotion. Flee from idolatry by seeking the Lord and His kingdom. As Peter Lord once said, *"The main thing is to keep the main thing the main thing."*

CHAPTER TWENTY-ONE

LOVE

As we begin our study of the individual characteristics of the fruit of the Spirit listed in Galatians 5:22-23, we need to remember that this is exactly what they are—individual characteristics of the "fruit" of the Spirit, singular, not "fruits," plural. If we have one, we should have them all. If we lose one, we will lose them all. They are inseparable.

This is not a matter of being overly technical. It is important that we understand the unity of diversity that is the nature of the Spirit. If we have the Spirit, we should have all of His characteristics or fruit in our lives. Even so, we will study these characteristics separately, while also seeking to understand how they are interrelated and build on one another.

As we look at love, the first characteristic of the fruit of the Spirit listed, it is understandable that there has been almost an endless number of books written about the subject. Certainly, we will be learning about God's love for eternity, and even that will not be long enough! Even though we can only do a very cursory study of this great subject in this format, we must start with the unfathomable, God's love, because that is where all true love begins.

The ultimate demonstration of God's love is the cross. Again, the whole creation marvels at the cross, and we, too, will certainly be marveling at it forever. As we see in the Book of Revelation, because of this it seems that the ultimate title of the Son of God will always be "the Lamb." Who can truly behold the cross and not be overwhelmed by the love of God? That God would give His own Son, and that the Son would leave all of His glory in heaven to become a man, and to endure all that He did for our redemption and salvation, will forever be the greatest demonstration of God's love and character.

Because of this, who could truly behold this and not love Him? This is why the Apostle Paul, after many years of some of the greatest missionary service of all time, acknowledged that the secret of His success was simply preaching the cross. There will never be anything that describes God more than the cross, and the message is love. There is nothing so compelling, so overwhelming in its breadth and depth, so beyond anything that mere men could have ever devised.

Even Napoleon, when he read the Gospel of John, remarked that if Jesus was not the Son of God, then the one who wrote that Gospel was because he knew men, and no man could have ever come up with a story like that! If anything, the Gospel story is unbelievable because it is so much higher than anything man can comprehend, and we can only see it "through a glass darkly" in this life. However, to see and to believe is the highest purpose to which we can attain in this life.

Even beginning to comprehend this love of God revealed by the cross will have such a profound impact on any life that it will cause the person to start life all over again, being born-again. Life in the light of the cross is radically different than any other life that we could lead on this earth. Because of it, everything changes. When we truly behold the cross and the sacrifice that He made for us, we cannot help but to love Him and pursue a similar life of sacrifice, desiring to do all things for Him, and for the sake of the gospel that testifies of this great love.

To truly begin beholding the cross, the most selfless act on the part of the greatest Being, the Creator Himself, cannot help but to unravel the selfishness of the fallen human nature. The more clearly we behold the cross and the love of God, the more sacrificial we will be in our own lives. The true Christian life is a life of sacrifice, a life of the cross. This the Lord Himself made clear in Matthew 16:24-25:

> **Then Jesus said to His disciples, "If anyone wishes to come after Me, let him deny himself, and take up his cross, and follow Me.**
>
> **"For whoever wishes to save his life shall lose it; but whoever loses his life for My sake shall find it."**

True love is the opposite of self-seeking. It is focusing on the interests of others more than ourselves. True love is focused first and foremost on the interests of God. Only by living for and in the love of God can we do that which is truly in the best interests of anyone else, including ourselves.

Loving God is the first and most important commandment, which we must endeavor to always keep first. If we love anyone or anything above God, then we have made them or it an idol. If we do not love the Lord more than we love anyone else, we will not love anyone else the way that we should. Remember, *"the main thing is to keep the main thing the main thing,"* and loving God is the main thing that we were created for. It is our highest attainment, and the love for God is our most valuable possession.

"We love, because He first loved us" (I John 4:19). How can we ever behold Him and not love Him? There really is no being in the universe more lovable than God. The more we get to know Him, the more we will love Him. As we are told in I John 4:16,

> **And we have come to know and have believed the love which God has for us. God is love, and the one who abides in love abides in God, and God abides in him.**

If we are truly getting to know God better, we will love more. We will love Him more, and we will love others more as well, as we are also assured in I John 4:20-21,

> **If someone says, "I love God," and hates his brother, he is a liar; for the one who does not love his brother whom he has seen, cannot love God whom he has not seen.**

And this commandment we have from Him, that the one who loves God should love his brother also.

There are different kinds of love and different degrees of love, but without question, love should be a primary pursuit of every Christian, just as we are told in the chapter that many believe to be the greatest in the Bible, I Corinthians 13, Paul's great discourse describing just what love is. It may not be possible to do this better than the great Apostle, and it just would not be fitting to do any study on love without considering it; therefore, I quote it below for your convenience:

If I speak with the tongues of men and of angels, but do not have love, I have become a noisy gong or a clanging cymbal.

And if I have the gift of prophecy, and know all mysteries and all knowledge; and if I have all faith, so as to remove mountains, but do not have love, I am nothing.

And if I give all my possessions to feed the poor, and if I deliver my body to be burned, but do not have love, it profits me nothing.

Love is patient, love is kind, and is not jealous; love does not brag and is not arrogant,

does not act unbecomingly; it does not seek its own, is not provoked, does not take into account a wrong suffered,

does not rejoice in unrighteousness, but rejoices with the truth;

bears all things, believes all things, hopes all things, endures all things.

Love never fails; but if there are gifts of prophecy, they will be done away; if there are tongues, they will cease; if there is knowledge, it will be done away.

For we know in part, and we prophesy in part;

but when the perfect comes, the partial will be done away.

When I was a child, I used to speak as a child, think as a child, reason as a child; when I became a man, I did away with childish things.

For now we see in a mirror dimly, but then face to face; now I know in part, but then I shall know fully just as I also have been fully known.

But now abide faith, hope, love, these three; but the greatest of these is love.

What more could be said?

CHAPTER TWENTY-TWO

JOY

This study may seem out of place after witnessing so much suffering from the Katrina disaster. However, I think the timing is perfect. It is the joy of the Lord that is our strength in any situation, and we can and should have joy in Him in any and every situation.

Let us also consider that this kind of suffering is going on every day in our world, though most of it is not in a place where the media can focus on it and, therefore, it does not get the attention or the aid that the Katrina victims are receiving. This is not to imply that the attention on Katrina is not warranted; it is, but the answer is not to let our hearts and minds be controlled by the conditions on earth, but by the conditions in heaven so that we can bring heaven's answers into any condition on the earth.

Because joy is a characteristic of the Holy Spirit, it should be a characteristic of all who have the Spirit. This does not mean that Christians cannot at times feel sorrow, grief, or even anger, but we should be primarily joyful, with these being the exceptions due to exceptional circumstances. If there is more sorrow, anger, or grief in our lives than joy, then we are not abiding in the Holy Spirit as we should.

Now let's apply this to some very real and present situations, such as natural disasters, pandemics, and other terrible problems that come cascading down on the world almost continuously. How can we be joyful in the midst of all of these tragedies?

First, the joy of the Holy Spirit comes with the grace and dignity of the Holy Spirit that would never be insensitive to someone else's sufferings. In fact, we are told that if one member of the body suffers we should suffer with them (see I Corinthians 12:26). We are also told in a number of places that the Lord Himself shares our sufferings. If He shares them and He is all-powerful, why doesn't He just do something about them? If He did, the whole experience of this world and this life would have no meaning.

As we are told in Psalm 115:16, **"The heavens are the heavens of the Lord, but the earth He has given to the sons of men."** The Lord gave authority over the earth to men. He will not intervene unless we ask Him to, which is usually not until we have botched things so badly that they are far out of our control. He is still gracious and merciful enough to very often intervene. All of the troubles at the end of this age will be the result of mankind determining to live without God. When we have botched this world to the degree that all life on the planet is in jeopardy, He will intervene. Even so, we need to understand that the great problems we are facing are not His fault, but ours. Our salvation begins with the humility to admit this, which is called repentance.

Christians, who have built their houses upon the Rock, which is to both hear and obey the Words of the Lord, have a kingdom which cannot be shaken. There is a joy that we should have because we know the King, and we know that He has authority over all things. He will also cause all things to work together for good for His people, so that even though we are temporarily hurting, we have an even more profound joy that makes our suffering far more bearable. Though we, too, suffer at times, we have a hope that we know will never disappoint us.

Again, we also need to keep in mind that the fruit of the Spirit is called fruit because it is cultivated and grown. How do we grow joy in our lives? First, we plant seeds, we water them, we keep them weeded, and we protect them until the fruit appears and matures. If we have a problem with depression, we should focus even more on the things that bring us the joy of the Lord.

If you have a problem with depression, do not read tragic stories or watch tragic programs all of the time. As compelling as the news may be, do not overly focus on it. Watch over the seeds that are sown in your heart and mind. Our news media hardly knows how to cover anything positive, and those who are getting most of their information from the news media will naturally be depressed and increasingly subject to fear and panic attacks.

Do not focus on your own personal tragedies as much, but determine that you are going to thank the Lord for everything He has allowed in your life because it is sure to bring good. I would watch or read many comedies for every tragedy. Laughter is one of the wonderful gifts that God has given to us, and we need to do it often. As we are told in Proverbs 17:22, **"A joyful heart is good medicine."** There is healing in joy!

Deuteronomy 28:47-48 is very enlightening concerning the power of joy, and the consequences of not having it: **"Because you did not serve the Lord your God with joy and a glad heart, for the abundance of all things; therefore you shall serve your enemies...."** Or this could be phrased: If we do not serve the Lord with joy, we will end up going into bondage. This is why "holy laughter" actually resulted in many people getting healed and freed from yokes of bondage.

In I Chronicles 12, we read how much joy there was in Israel when David was made king over all Israel. Likewise, all of heaven rejoices when a single person submits to the Lordship of Jesus. The greatest joy of all will be when the King comes to establish His authority over the earth. We can begin to have and spread this joy as we submit our lives to His will.

There is a reason why the Lord commanded much more feasting than fasting. If the people are joyful, it is a reflection on the leadership of those in authority. Therefore, the joy of the Lord's people should be profound and contagious. The greatest joy of all is that even the worst problems and tragedies on this earth are temporary. The King is going to come back to establish His kingdom, and when He does He promises that there will be no more mourning, crying, pain, or death. How can we not be continually in awe and wonder at our God? How can we not be far more profoundly joyful than sorrowful, unless it is that we have allowed the cares of this present world to choke out our knowledge and vision of eternity?

We have a God who has authority over all. He is far more full of kindness, mercy, and benevolence than even the greatest human king, and He is coming back to set everything right! How can we fail to rejoice in Him?

CHAPTER TWENTY-THREE

PEACE

"Blessed are the peacemakers, for they shall be called sons of God" (Matthew 5:9).

Since the time when there were just two brothers on the entire planet, they had trouble getting along. One of them basically said, "This world is not big enough for the both of us!" Since then there has been conflict between men. One of the primary reasons why the Lord came was to bring peace to the earth, which is one of the primary reasons His people are here as we read in Luke 1:68-79, one of the most comprehensive statements in Scripture of the purpose of the Messiah:

"Blessed be the Lord God of Israel, for He has visited us and accomplished redemption for His people,

and has raised up a horn of salvation for us in the house of David His servant—

as He spoke by the mouth of His holy prophets from of old—

salvation from our enemies, and from the hand of all who hate us;

to show mercy toward our fathers, and to remember His holy covenant,

the oath which He swore to Abraham our father,

to grant us that we, being delivered from the hand of our enemies, might serve Him without fear,

in holiness and righteousness before Him all our days.

"And you, child, will be called the prophet of the Most High; for you will go on before the Lord to prepare His ways;

to give to His people the knowledge of salvation by the forgiveness of their sins,

because of the tender mercy of our God, with which the Sunrise from on high shall visit us,

to shine upon those who sit in darkness and the shadow of death, to guide our feet into the way of peace."

The conclusion of all that He came to do was to **"guide our feet into the way of peace."** For this reason, we should examine our walk to see if this has in fact been something that we have been growing in, and is the fruit that we are leaving behind. As Ephesians 2:17 states, **"And He came and preached** peace to you who were far away, and peace to those who were near." We also see this in the very first heavenly proclamation of His birth, recorded in Luke 2:13-14:

> And suddenly there appeared with the angel a multitude of the heavenly host praising God, and saying,

> "Glory to God in the highest, and on earth peace among men with whom He is pleased."

Since this is so basic to the reason why the Lord came to the earth, it should be one of the primary characteristics of those who have partaken of His redemption. He is even called the **"Prince of Peace," (see Isaiah 9:6)** so those over whom He truly reigns will be examples of this peace.

However, the Lord's peace is not like the world's peace. The world's peace is based on compromise and human alliances which have never been found strong enough to last. His peace is based on His authority to rule, and to bring mankind and the rest of creation into harmony through Himself. There is no lasting peace outside of Him, and at the conclusion of this age, it will be demonstrated for all of creation for all of eternity that He alone is the answer to our problems. True peace can only be found by coming back into harmony with God and His will.

In the rising conflict and confusion, His peace will be demonstrated by His people, and it will stand in increasing contrast to the conflicts and confusion. By His grace and mercy, in the midst of all that is coming, He will make His peace available to all who will come to Him. If we are wise, we will come to Him now. If we claim to know Him but do not have His peace, then we do not know Him as we should. Now is the time to find Him and His peace. His peace is stronger than any human problem and any chaos.

Again, if we are abiding in the Lord, we will also be manifesting His character, which is the fruit of the Spirit. Therefore, all Christians should have as a primary vision for their lives to grow in the fruit of the Spirit. Many do have a devotion to growing in love, which is called the greatest of these, and certainly this is a right thing to do. We should also have as a primary vision to grow in the peace of God.

Peace is actually the linchpin fruit of the Spirit that holds all of the others together. If you lose your peace, you are going to also quickly lose your patience, gentleness, self-control, and so on. That is why most of the devil's attacks against us are directed at stealing our peace first. If he can get us anxious and fretting, he will, at the very least, be able to push us far from the will of God in our lives.

Many Christians do allow their worries to dictate the course of their lives even more than the Spirit of God. Worry or anxiety is not a fruit of the Spirit, and the Lord will never lead us with it. Dissatisfaction and discontent are not the fruit of the Spirit, and if we allow them to dictate what we do, they, too, will actually drive us far from the will of God in our lives. If we are going to follow the Spirit, we will abide in the fruit of the Spirit, which is: "**...love, joy, peace, patience, kindness, goodness, faithfulness, gentleness, self-control" (see Galatians 5:22-23).**

The title "Lord of hosts," which means "Lord of armies," is used to describe the Lord over ten times more than all of the other titles used for the Lord. He is a martial God. To really understand Him we must understand His military characteristics. Likewise, His people are called to be His army as well as His bride. However, it is not "the Lord of hosts" who it says crushes Satan under our feet, but rather "**...the God of peace will soon crush Satan under your feet" (see Romans 16:20).** It is by abiding in the peace of God that the devil's inroads into our lives, "the gates of hell," are shut and he is utterly crushed.

As the world grows in fear, those who know God will be growing in peace. We will not understand the time or the course we should take without abiding in His peace, because without His peace we are not abiding in His Spirit, Who alone can lead us into the truth. This is why we must learn now to obey the great apostolic exhortation in Philippians 4:4-7:

> **Rejoice in the Lord always; again I will say, rejoice!**

> **Let your forbearing spirit be known to all men. The Lord is near.**

Be anxious for nothing, but in everything by prayer and supplication with thanksgiving let your requests be made known to God.

And the peace of God, which surpasses all comprehension, shall guard your hearts and your minds in Christ Jesus.

As we see here, it is **"the peace of God"** that guards our hearts and minds and keeps them in Christ Jesus. We must learn to quickly recognize anything that is attacking our peace and trying to steal it. We should resolve that every time the devil tries to steal our peace, we are going to grow in peace because it will be a great opportunity to do that. The very thing that would steal our peace if we let it, will strengthen our peace if we resist it.

The peace of God is rooted in trusting in the Lord. We have peace because we know who He is, the King of kings, who is over all rule and authority and dominion. We trust His authority and know that nothing can touch us unless He allows it. We trust Him to know that anything He allows is for our good, as He has promised in His Word, which is sure, as we read in Romans 8:28:

And we know that God causes all things to work together for good to those who love God, to those who are called according to His purpose.

It is for this purpose that we can, as the exhortation above encourages us, **"Rejoice in the Lord**

always" and **"be anxious for nothing."** We can have joy in everything, even our trials, because we know that He is causing everything to work for our good. Those who trust will not be anxious. Those who trust will let their forbearing spirit or patience be known to all because they will stand out in stark contrast to the fears and worries that are coming upon those who do not have this faith.

The highest purpose of man is to be the dwelling place of God. If we abide in Him, He will abide in us. This should, therefore, be the highest goal of each of us. It should be the greatest focus that we have every day. The true success of our lives in every way will be dependent on this one thing. It is for this reason that we should seek to understand the dwelling places of God in Scripture, because they are each a revelation of the characteristics of the ones He will dwell in. Of special note is the fact that after entering the Promised Land, God's dwelling place was Shiloh, which means "peace." The only place to which He ever moved was Jerusalem, which means "city of peace." Obviously, this is a revelation of a basic characteristic He seeks in those with whom He will dwell—peace.

All of the metaphors that the Lord uses in Scripture are chosen because they are a revelation to us of His ways and purposes. It is no accident that the Lord chose a dove to be the symbol of the Holy Spirit that was to abide with Jesus and with us. Doves are some of the most sensitive of all birds. They are also very selective about where they will land, choosing only quiet, peaceful places. You will never find doves nesting around places that have a lot of commotion.

Pigeons, which are related to doves, are not like this, but will settle just about anywhere or on anyone who will feed them. The Holy Spirit is not a pigeon! As R. T. Kendall stated so well, few can discern between a true move of the Holy Spirit and "pigeon religion." Therefore, many Christians will flock to and land on just about anything, but those who know the Holy Spirit will not be like that.

It is noteworthy that the Lord told over five hundred people who had seen Him after His resurrection to go and wait for the promise of the Father in Jerusalem, but on the day that the Holy Spirit came, there were only one hundred twenty left. Of the one hundred twenty on the Day of Pentecost, it was said that "they were in one accord," in unity, or at peace with one another. Peace and unity are more important than numbers when seeking to attract the Holy Spirit. As our friend Francis Frangipane likes to say, "In prayer four of a kind beats a full house."

We often seek to gather as many people as we can to us because most do get their encouragement from numbers. However, it is a repeated witness of history that most great moves of the Holy Spirit began in small groups who were in unity and focused on one purpose. Of course, when the Holy Spirit begins to move, many will be drawn. However, many such moves are short-lived because it is easy to be distracted by the desires of the people, rather than keeping our attention on what attracted the Holy Spirit.

Peace is a basic requirement for the place where the Lord will dwell because it will be through His dwelling place that He will bring peace to the earth. We see this in the great promise that the Lord gave concerning His restored house in Haggai 2:9:

> **"The latter glory of this house will be greater than the former," says the Lord of hosts, "and in this place I shall give peace...."**

We see this also in Psalm 122:6-9:

> **Pray for the peace of Jerusalem: "May they prosper who love you.**

> **"May peace be within your walls, and prosperity within your palaces."**

> **For the sake of my brothers and my friends, I will now say, "May peace be within you."**

> **For the sake of the house of the Lord our God I will seek your good.**

God is repeatedly called **"the God of Peace"** in the New Testament, and as we have already studied, it is **"the God of Peace"** who crushes Satan under our feet (see Romans 16:20). If we abide in the peace of God, it will utterly crush the devil's work wherever we go. This is why we are told in Ephesians 6:15 that our feet are to be shod with **"the gospel of peace."** The peace of God is a basic counter to the spirit of this world that is always seeking to spread strife and conflict. For this reason, Paul wrote the important exhortation in Romans 14:17-19:

> **For the kingdom of God is not eating and drinking, but righteousness and peace and joy in the Holy Spirit.**
>
> **For he who in this way serves Christ is acceptable to God and approved by men.**
>
> **So then let us pursue the things which make for peace and the building up of one another.**

Many are in the continual pursuit of joy, but seldom find it because they do not take the path that leads to true joy, which is first the pursuit of righteousness, or doing what is right. Then peace and righteousness together bring true joy. As we are told in this text, this is the kingdom of God or how we enter the kingdom. We are also told that the way we build up one another is by pursuing the things that make for peace. Peace itself is an edifying factor. In this world, which is increasingly hurried and in increasing discord, the peace of God will be an increasingly dramatic contrast to the world and an increasing treasure to those who find it.

Another remarkable verse in Scripture about peace is found in Hebrews 12:14: **"Pursue peace with all men, and the sanctification without which no one will see the Lord."** Think about this. We are told to pursue peace with **"all men,"** not just those who are a part of our fellowship or even our faith. This does not mean that we will have peace with all men, but it should be a basic devotion of ours, and it is so important we do this if we expect to **"see the Lord."**

The following verse, 15, says, **"See to it that no one comes short of the grace of God; that no root of bitterness springing up causes trouble, and by it many be defiled."** In my studies of church history, it seems that the majority of false teachings, or those who brought divisions to the church, are mostly influenced by a wound or rejection that causes the one wounded or rejected to form their teachings in reaction to this. Of course, such can usually find Scriptures which will concur with their teachings when taken out of context or distorted, but it is easy for those who know the true peace of God to discern such bitterness and roots of bitterness. Usually those who are attracted to such movements or teachings are only those who are likewise wounded.

True Christianity is founded on forgiveness. Only when we forgive will we have peace, not doing or teaching the things which cause division in the church. We must pursue peace in order to see the Lord because He is the Prince of Peace. If we see Him, we will see His peace. If we are abiding in Him, we will have His peace.

Hebrews 12:14 also addresses the required sanctification that we must have in order to see the Lord. This is linked to pursuing peace because, as we are told in I Thessalonians 5:23 and II Peter 3:14, it is the **"God of peace"** who sanctifies us. It is not possible to live a truly holy life without abiding in the Lord's peace.

Legalism, which many confuse with true holiness, is a life of striving and worry that one has fallen short somehow, while true holiness is based on a profound trust in the work of the cross of Jesus, and a love for Him that compels us to want to please Him in all things. True holiness is motivated out of a love for God, not a fear of punishment. It is true that the fear of the Lord is the beginning of wisdom, but it is not the mature conclusion of wisdom, which is love.

As we are told in Ephesians 2:14, Jesus is our peace. There is no true peace on this earth aside from Him, and this will become increasingly apparent in the time ahead. As He sits in the heavens, above all rule and authority and dominion, He is never worried or shaken with even the worst things that take place on the earth. If we abide in Him, we, too, will have perfect peace in all things. This should be a primary goal of all Christians in all circumstances. In all things, do not focus on the problem, but the Solution, the Lord Himself, and you will have peace.

In Philippians 4:7, we are told that it is the **"peace of God"** that guards our hearts and minds in Christ Jesus. Do not let anything steal your peace. The peace of God is not mentioned as one of the greater gifts, but, as discussed, it is the one that holds all of them together. If you lose your peace, you will lose your patience, love, and so on. Now we want to discuss a bit more practically how this happens.

The Zone

When I was once asked to speak to a conference of professional athletes, I happened upon a very interesting and insightful study that I thought articulated this about as well as it could be in practical terms. The author of this article was a psychologist who had studied for over twenty years what athletes call "the zone." The zone is a place of super performance where even the best athletes reach a level that is beyond their usually great abilities. When they get into the zone they feel unstoppable, and often are.

What athletes call "the zone" is very much like the Spirit that we are called to abide in, where we accomplish things that are far beyond our own abilities, and are, in fact, unstoppable as long as we abide in the Spirit. That is what the normal Christian life should be, and that should be a basic devotion that we have—to live in the Spirit.

The author of this article about the zone was never able to determine what enabled athletes to get into that place of super performance, but he was able to determine what would bring them out of it—either fear or anger. I believe that these are also the two main attacks that the devil sends against us to keep us from living in the Spirit. As was cited in this study, a single moment of terror or rage consumes as much of the energy in the body as many hours of hard labor. This is why after you have been through a big scare or have become really angry, you will then tend to feel tired. If you are just an anxious worrier, or a bitter, angry person, you are consuming the energy of your body at a much faster rate, and will, therefore, tend to be tired a lot because of it.

Creative people, and those who accomplish great things, are usually operating at a level of 10 percent, or even more, above those who just exist. The super performers practice, study, and in other ways prepare, and then perform at a level that is only a little more than those who do not. If we are angry or fearful people, more than 10 percent of our energy is being sapped from us, and it is keeping us from accomplishing what we could.

As this author noted, if an opposing player gets into the zone and can either be intimidated or become angry, he will come out of it. If you, yourself, get into the zone, he recommends guarding against these two things so you can stay in that level of super performance. This is good advice for Christians, too. When we begin to walk in the Spirit and get used by God, the devil will try to get us to worry, fear something, or become angry. These things are sapping the life of true accomplishment from many Christians. We must, therefore, guard against fear or anxiety, anger, and unforgiveness.

In one of my favorite Psalms, and one of the greatest exhortations in Scripture about how we inherit the promises of God, we read:

Do not fret because of evildoers, be not envious toward wrongdoers.

For they will wither quickly like the grass, and fade like the green herb.

Trust in the Lord, and do good; dwell in the land and cultivate faithfulness.

Delight yourself in the Lord; and He will give you the desires of your heart.

Commit your way to the Lord, trust also in Him, and He will do it.

And He will bring forth your righteousness as the light, and your judgment as the noonday.

Rest in the Lord and wait patiently for Him. Do not fret because of him who prospers in his way, because of the man who carries out wicked schemes.

Cease from anger, and forsake wrath; do not fret, it leads only to evildoing.

For evildoers will be cut off, but those who wait for the Lord, they will inherit the land (Psalm 37:1-9).

We see here at the beginning of the great Psalm about inheriting the promises of God, we are told not to worry and to forsake anger. These two enemies can keep us from our inheritance!

This is why learning to abide in the peace of God is so crucial. This is also why it is the peace of God that will trample the devil's attacks on us. This is why, in the armor of God, our feet are to be shod with **"the gospel of peace" (see Ephesians 6:15)**. The peace of God is one of our greatest weapons. Use it by abiding in it. Do not let anything steal your peace.

Again, this is why the dwelling places of God in Scripture in the Promised Land were Shiloh, which was from a word many interpreted as "peace," and Jerusalem, which means "city of peace." Obviously, this is a revelation of a basic characteristic He seeks in those whom He will dwell with—peace. This is also how we abide in Him, by entering His peace.

The earth itself, and governments throughout it, are experiencing more and more of the prophesied shaking that is to come until everything that can be shaken will be shaken, but we have a kingdom that cannot be shaken. This is going to be one of the primary ways that those who are the true representatives of the kingdom will be distinguished in the times ahead from all others. We do not need to worry; the kingdom of God is at hand. Resist fear. Resist anger. Do not let anything steal your peace.

CHAPTER TWENTY-FOUR

PATIENCE

A few years ago I had a dream in which I was mountain climbing with many thousands of people. Hundreds were all connected together by the lifelines that mountain climbers use. Many were falling off of the mountain and being lost because some were not driving their stakes deep enough into the ground. If one gave way, often many were lost. I knew in the dream that those stakes were truth. For that reason, in every study I do and in all of my writings, I try to drive the stakes of truth as deep as I can into the ground. That is also the purpose for so much repetition and review in these studies.

If you will develop this strategy in your life, going deeper and deeper into sound, biblical truth, you will not only be stronger and more secure in the Lord because of it, but it may save your spiritual life, as well as others whom you are connected to. This type of devotion will be needed more and more in the times ahead. We are studying the fruit of the Spirit, in depth, for this reason. If you are abiding in the Lord, you will have His nature.

To abide and grow in the fruit of the Spirit will be a fortress for our souls, but even more, it will position us to be used more by the Lord. We are not here just to make it through this life—we are here to prevail over the enemy and set his captives free. In John 17:18, the Lord Jesus said to the Father, **"As You sent Me into the world, I also have sent them into the world."** (**NKJV**) The purpose for which He was sent into the world was to destroy the works of the devil (see I John 3:8). The primary way that the works of the devil are destroyed in our own lives is by abiding in the Holy Spirit. Once we have overcome evil in our own lives, we can then be used to set others free.

So, our goal is not to just study this fruit, but to grow in it. This study will help our understanding of the prophecies of the end times because, until we are abiding in the Spirit and following the Spirit, we will not really be able to understand what these prophecies mean, much less be properly prepared by them.

This leads us to the next fruit of the Spirit listed in Galatians 5:22: **"patience."** As we have stated, there is actually one fruit of the Spirit, and these are all characteristics of it. Therefore, they are all linked and intertwined. If we really have one, we will have the others as well. Even so, Scripture links faith and patience, especially in Hebrews 6:11-12:

> **And we desire that each one of you show the same diligence so as to realize the full assurance of hope until the end,**

that you may not be sluggish, but imitators of those who through faith and patience inherit the promises.

If this is true, and we know that it is, why is it we have this huge, worldwide "faith movement," but have never heard of a "patience movement?" Certainly this may be the least popular, least written and preached about, and least practiced characteristic of the fruit of the Spirit. This is likely the cause of many of the problems that so many Christians go through.

True faith is possibly most demonstrated by patience. Wasn't that how faith was demonstrated by Abraham, "the father of faith?" He was too old when God called him, and yet the Lord made him wait about twenty more years for the heir to be born in his own house. Abraham was made to wait until it was physically impossible for him, until his faith was not in himself, but in the Lord, as it is written in Romans 4:18: "who, contrary to hope, believed in hope, so that he became the father of many nations" (literal translation).

Any normal, natural hope was actually contrary to Abraham's faith. True faith is not natural, but is often contrary to all other circumstances, including time. However, with the passage of time, true faith will grow stronger, while pretentious faith will wither. This is a reason why, just as Israel experienced, between the place where we receive the promises of God and the Promised Land, there is usually a wilderness that is the exact opposite of what we were promised. As we are told in I Corinthians 10:1-11, this was done for our instruction upon whom the ends of the ages have come. It is this wilderness, which requires our patience, where not only is our faith perfected, but we are matured in every way that we will need to be proper stewards of the promises.

The church's lack of patience has shown up in recent years in the way it has been susceptible to the most outrageous "get rich quick" schemes. Many churches and ministries have fallen prey to these, losing millions of dollars to them, and some even losing millions to each one. These schemes all seem to feed on the popular hope that the wealth of the wicked is going to be given to the righteous, which is a biblical hope, as we see in Proverbs 13:22, "**...the wealth of the sinner is stored up for the righteous.**"

There are other biblical prophecies that speak of the wealth of the nations being given to the righteous. There is no question that this will come to pass, but it is important to determine who are the righteous and who are the sinners. It was the faith of Abraham, demonstrated by his remarkable patience, which was attributed to him as righteousness.

We should actually be wary of things that happen for us too fast or too easily. Wasn't that the root of the devil's temptation of Jesus? When the devil promised Jesus all of the kingdoms of the earth if He would just bow down and worship him, what he was offering the Lord was the easy, quick way to receive what He had been promised, without the pain of the cross. That is still a primary way the devil tempts God's chosen vessels to depart from their true calling.

In Scripture, one can sense a distinction between wealth and riches. Riches, which may come fast or easily, **"makes itself wings" (see Proverbs 23:5),** or leaves just as fast and easily. True wealth is the result of true righteousness, which will always be demonstrated by diligence, faithfulness, and endurance. It is lasting, and will even pass on to future generations.

Recently, I was intrigued by a study done on those who had won the lottery. Of the hundreds who had become instant millionaires, most were broke again very fast, having foolishly thrown their money away. Just a year or two after winning the lottery, they were in worse shape than they had been before winning the lottery. They no longer had jobs; they had alienated many friends and relatives, and many had even lost their homes. Of all of the people they had researched, there did not seem to be a single one who had a happy ending, even among the Christians who had won. Overall, it seemed that winning the lottery could be one of the worst things that could happen to anyone.

The wilderness and the patience required to get through it are for the purpose of changing our fallen nature into His nature, perfecting our character, and teaching us the wisdom needed to manage the blessings of the Promised Land. Few things will demonstrate true faith as will patience. Godly wisdom is always linked to patience. It was the source of Abraham's faith, and ours too, if it is authentic. The passage of time strengthens true faith and exposes the false.

It has been said that the devil knows he has only a short time left, so he is always in a hurry. The Lord knows that He has eternity, so He is never in a hurry. Obviously, those who are abiding in the Lord are not going to be in a hurry. If we have the true peace of God and the true faith of God, it will be demonstrated by patience. Carl Jung, one of the fathers of modern psychotherapy, once wrote that "Hurry is not of the devil—it is the devil!" He said this because of the obvious ability that impatience has to distort and pervert human character.

Have you ever wondered why the Scriptures are so full of exhortations to wait upon God, but there is not a single one that tells us to hurry? It is obvious that we tend to have a problem with patience.

We also now live in a time that seems especially devoted to attacking patience. From fast foods to fast planes, "fast" is now a commodity with increasing value, as the saying "Time is money" stresses. I have run into Christian leaders who said they no longer believed in prophecy because their prophetic promises had not come to pass, and it had been over six months! You have to wonder if such people have ever read the Bible. As the Scriptures make clear, and wise saints know well, anything that comes too fast, or too easily, is insignificant.

Moses spent forty years in the wilderness before God called him. The Apostle Paul went into the wilderness and spent what some have estimated to be fourteen years just getting his message from the Lord. As he wrote to the Galatians, he was waiting for the Lord to be revealed *in him*, not just *to him*. There is a big difference.

When we are driven by a sense that we are running out of time, we obviously are not abiding in the Lord, who has eternity and is never in a hurry. Because we are a publisher, we are often bombarded by more manuscripts than we could ever read. I have, therefore, asked the Lord to help me discern the ones that have merit that we should consider. One of the things that I was shown to look for as evidence we should not waste our time considering a manuscript was an author's "sense of urgency." Not only are such inevitably superficial, but they also promote superficial faith and superficial vision.

There is no question that depth and wisdom come with the passage of time. The older and wiser we get, if we have stayed on course, the more patience we will have. However, sometimes patience can become an excuse for inaction or lukewarmness. To those who are lukewarm or led more by fear than by faith, just getting them moving at all can be a task, so I never preach about patience in a church that is lukewarm or fearful. Those who are not doing anything do not need to be patient—they need to be raised from the dead! Even so, impatience is not a fruit of the Spirit, and if we are led by our impatience, we will not be led by the Spirit, and we will not be found doing the Lord's will.

CHAPTER TWENTY-FIVE

KINDNESS

The next fruit of the Spirit listed in Galatians 5 is **"kindness."** This is defined as being considerate, generous, and benevolent. It is the character trait that is the opposite of selfishness, but is rather the nature of one who is thinking of others.

Kindness is basically the opposite of the fallen nature of man. After the first transgression, Adam and Eve immediately looked at themselves, and self-centeredness has been one of the basic characteristics of fallen man since. However, kindness causes us to be more considerate of others, looking out for their interests.

Kindness is the opposite of being harsh. It is a thoughtful, generous demeanor that does not tend to overreact and is not prone to think the worst about others, but the best. How different would the world be if everyone became kind toward one another, always regarding others in the best light instead of the worst, and always being generous in their dealings with one another? How would the church be different? How would our families be different?

Because this is a "fruit of the Spirit," kindness is a very basic characteristic of the nature of God and will be a basic characteristic of His kingdom that is coming. So, those who are helping to prepare the way for His kingdom will have this as a very basic character trait as well. Kindness is such a radical contrast to the nature of people that any who are truly kind will stand out like a great light. This is our calling. If we are not standing out in this way, then we are not as spiritual as we think, regardless of how much knowledge we have.

Think about the last thing that someone did that really upset you. Now think about how you would have reacted if kindness was a basic part of your nature. Would you have done anything differently? For most of us, the answer would be "yes." If the people you know were asked to think of the kindest people they know, would you be one who comes to mind? If not, how do we get there? How do we change?

Many think that not acting on their feelings in a situation is dishonest, or being fake. However, this is not dishonest, but rather the pursuit of transformation. As we have discussed, this is called "the fruit of the Spirit," because like fruit, it must be cultivated and grown. To bear fruit a tree must be planted, watered, and protected while it is growing. Then, after it begins to bear fruit, it must be pruned by cutting off the branches that are not bearing fruit.

Just as the Lord created man to have fellowship with Him and to cultivate the garden, the cultivation of the garden of our hearts is accomplished the same way. The Lord will walk with us in it, but He also expects us to do a lot of the work. It is a partnership. The Holy Spirit is the one working with us in transformation, but we, too, have a part to play. How do we do our part?

First, we discern through our fellowship with the Lord what He wants cultivated in our lives. Then, as in the Parable of the Sower, we determine the threats to the seed that has been planted in us by the Word of God, and we protect it until there is fruit. If our hearts are good soil there will be fruit, but if we are careless, which means to care less, the seed is likely to be stolen so that there is no fruit.

The seed is the Word of God, and the watering of the seed is also from the Word of God. If we know that the Lord is working on cultivating kindness in us, we should be sensitive to this—being faithful to water this seed with His Word by taking the Scriptures about kindness and memorizing them, quoting them over and over while considering how we should apply them in our everyday lives. We need to also consider how to guard it from threats, such as the devil's attempts to steal it, shallowness on our part, and the cares and worries of this world that would choke out the seed.

Most of us still have several hundred things wrong with us that need changing, and it is the devil's strategy to try to get us to work on all of them at once, knowing that if we do this we will quickly be worn out and defeated. In contrast to this, the Holy Spirit usually works on just one or two things at a time, knowing that victory in one area can create a breakthrough and momentum that translates into victories in many other areas. That's why this is the "fruit of the Spirit," singular, instead of nine "fruits" of the Spirit.

This is also why the Word of God exhorts us to pursue love, because if we are growing in love, we will be kind and patient with others. Therefore, the fruit of the Spirit is the basic characteristics of love. We are even told that "faith works by love." Even so, at times we need to focus more specifically on one or two of these character traits, such as abiding in the peace of God or just simply being kind to others. Proverbs 3:3 exhorts us: **"Do not let kindness and truth leave you; bind them around your neck, write them on the tablet of your heart."**

In that time, there were no vaults or safety deposit boxes, so people would hang their greatest treasures from their neck in a pouch. When someone read this proverb, they would, therefore, think that kindness and truth should be considered as their greatest treasures. If we considered kindness as one of our greatest treasures in this same way, we would never be careless with it or lose it when we felt offended. It would be too precious to cast off just for the sake of such things. How would the world be impacted today if every Christian did this?

In Romans 2:4 the Apostle Paul writes, **"...do you think lightly of the riches of His kindness and** forbearance and patience, not knowing that the kindness of God leads you to repentance?" If it is God's kindness that calls men to repentance, then this kindness being expressed through us will do the same for others. It may not be immediate, but kindness and generosity are powerful weapons against the evil strife of this world.

If strife, backbiting, selfish ambition, and other such things are having their way in our workplace, neighborhood, family, or church, kindness will be one of the most powerful weapons to overcome them. We must always keep in mind that we overcome evil with good. As we are told in Colossians 3:12-13:

> **And so, as those who have been chosen of God, holy and beloved, put on a heart of compassion, kindness, humility, gentleness and patience;**
>
> **bearing with one another, and forgiving each other, whoever has a complaint against anyone; just as the Lord forgave you, so also should you.**

If we are being confronted with evil strife, the Lord has probably allowed it so that we can grow in kindness. Do not waste your trials, but discern the purpose for them, and grow in the Lord through this great opportunity. In II Peter 1:5-7, we are given a progression of how we grow in the nature of the Lord:

Now for this very reason also, applying all diligence, in your faith supply moral excellence, and in your moral excellence, knowledge;

and in your knowledge, self-control, and in your self-control, perseverance, and in your perseverance, godliness;

and in your godliness, brotherly kindness, and in your brotherly kindness, [Christian] love.

As we see here, kindness is the last step before love. We might conclude that if this is something the Lord is dealing with us about, it is an encouraging sign of maturity. Of course, until we are like Jesus, and doing the works that He did, we still need to grow more in all of these character traits. True godly kindness is the hallmark of a truly spiritual and mature believer.

CHAPTER TWENTY-SIX

GOODNESS

The next aspect of the fruit of the Spirit is **"goodness."** The Greek word that is translated is *agathosune,* which is defined as "virtue" or "beneficence." This is still a very broad concept that I would like to narrow down a bit so that we can get our minds around it and practically apply it. However, we do need to keep in mind that it is a broad and expansive characteristic that every Christian should have.

We often think of goodness as the opposite of being evil, which has some application, but it is much more than that. It is more of a verb than a noun. True goodness is active and practical. It is far more than just having a bleeding heart for people's problems; it is doing something about them.

In Acts 10:38 it says, **"You know of Jesus of Nazareth, how God anointed Him with the Holy Spirit and with power, and how He went about doing good, and healing all who were oppressed by the devil; for God was with Him."** That is one of the best definitions of the Lord's ministry while He walked the earth. This is, in fact, what should be said of every

Christian. The Lord has not changed, and He is seeking to do the same things through His body, the church, that He did when He was physically walking the earth.

Jesus went about **"doing good"** because God was with Him, and God is good and loves to do good. He lives in us to use us to do good for others. Therefore, if we are united with Him in our hearts, we will have that same nature of always looking for how we can do good and how we can help others. The Holy Spirit is called "the Helper," because it is His basic nature to help. If we are truly "Spirit filled," we, too, will be filled with the nature of one who wants to help others by doing good.

We also have in this one verse in Acts a definition of how Jesus did good—He healed all who were oppressed of the devil and He did this by the power of the Holy Spirit, which as the verse concludes, was the evidence of God being with Him. True goodness is practical, and for anyone who is sick or has a loved one who is sick, there is nothing you can do for them that they would appreciate more than healing. That is why this was such a basic part of the Lord's ministry on the earth when He was here physically, and it is still one of the primary things He wants to do through His body.

Healing is another very expansive subject that we will study later, but for now we need to consider that it is basic to our calling as His representatives on the earth because it is basic to revealing His nature of wanting to do good for people. For those who are afflicted or oppressed in this way, healing is the most good that could be done for them.

As this is actually a study of the end of this age, the conditions that we can expect to unfold on the earth, and how we are to be prepared for them, growing in faith for healing is going to be increasingly critical for the church in these times. We are coming to the time when human remedies will fall far short of the emerging problems.

Medical science has done a wonderful job in many ways, greatly raising the health and quality of life for multitudes. It is right for doctors to be esteemed as one of the noblest professions, but medical science will not be able to cope with the things that are being released in the world. Remember, **"the harvest is the end of the age" (see Matthew 13:39).** The harvest is everything that has been sown in man coming to full maturity—the good and the evil and the consequences of each. Disease is going to be getting more powerful, and viruses are going to be mutating beyond the ability of any human remedy. We must come to know Jesus as our Healer, and we must be vessels that Jesus the Healer can use in these times. As diseases and the fear of them increase, this is one of the ways that the goodness of the Lord will shine brighter and brighter in the increasing darkness.

Because goodness is a basic characteristic of the fruit of the Spirit, those who are growing in the Lord will demonstrate an increasing desire and ability to do good for others. Consider this biblical exhortation:

But as for you, brethren, do not grow weary of doing good (II Thessalonians 3:13).

We are exhorted to **"not grow weary of doing good"** because it is something that we should expect to have to deal with. Weariness is not just a physical problem, but a spiritual one. We grow more weary when we start losing hope or feeling that our labor is not making much of a difference. As we see mammoth problems come upon the earth, which will seem to be multiplying in spite of our best efforts, there will be a tendency to become weary and lose hope. However, every soul that we can touch and do good for has infinite value, is greatly loved by the Lord, and is worth all of our efforts.

If there was a great king and you were able to save or rescue one of his children, wouldn't that be a great deed? As a father, I know how much I appreciate anyone who helps one of my children in any way. Our Father in heaven, the King over all kings, is likewise deeply appreciative of anything we do to help one another, as we are told in Hebrews 13:16, **"And do not neglect doing good and sharing; for with such sacrifices God is pleased."** One of the main things that will keep us from getting weary is doing what we do for the Lord even more than for the people.

We must love people and want to help them for their own sakes, but many that we help will not even express appreciation. Remember the ten blind men that the Lord healed? Only one even returned to thank Him. Can we expect more? However, if we are doing what we do for the Lord more than just for the people, we have our satisfaction in knowing how much He appreciates it.

And let us not lose heart in doing good, for in due time we shall reap if we do not grow weary.

So then, while we have opportunity, let us do good to all men, and especially to those who are of the household of the faith (Galatians 6:9-10).

Here we are encouraged not to lose heart in doing good because we will reap if we do not grow weary. There will be a reward and a harvest. However, just as a farmer does not plant a seed, water it, and then stand there waiting for the fruit, we, too, need to understand that the true work going on in people's hearts is often hidden for a long period of time, but there is going to be fruit from our work. This is why we are given the interesting exhortation in Ecclesiastes 11:4-6:

He who watches the wind will not sow and he who looks at the clouds will not reap.

Just as you do not know the path of the wind and how bones are formed in the womb of the pregnant woman, so you do not know the activity of God who makes all things.

Sow your seed in the morning, and do not be idle in the evening, for you do not know whether morning or evening sowing will succeed, or whether both of them alike will be good.

To state it more basically, we must not look too much at the outward conditions, but sow the seed of good works whenever and wherever we can, because we trust God to use them the way that He desires, and to bring forth the harvest. As Galatians 6:10 above states, **"while we have opportunity, let us do good to all men, and especially to those who are of the household of the faith."**

Practical Goodness

In Tolstoy's classic novel, *War and Peace,* Count Pierre is filled with compassion for his serfs and desperately wants to help them. He talks about it frequently, and sincerely wants to do it. His friend, Prince Andrey, is not motivated by compassion as much as he is sound business principles and good management, but because he runs his estates so efficiently his serfs are several times better off than Pierre's. Pierre certainly talked about helping the serfs more and really wanted to, but who did the most good?

In my opinion, this is pretty typical of the difference between liberal and conservative politics. In many areas, liberals have a right heart toward people and issues, but their remedy often leaves conditions actually worse and inevitably becomes a huge waste of resources. Conservatives, and those who are motivated more out of sound business and management principles, who often are simply wanting to develop more markets rather than having compassion, still actually do far more good for people. This is why Winston Churchill once said, "If you are not a liberal at twenty, you have no heart; if you are not a conservative at forty, you have no brain."

Government is prone toward bureaucratic remedies that will inevitably become so inefficient that only a fraction of the resources will actually get to the needy. The same has happened to many large charities and to many church programs and ministries. Can this be why the Lord, who certainly emphasized the condition of the heart, also taught a lot about pragmatic economics, such as with The Parable of the Talents.

There are far more references in Scripture about financial planning and management than any other subject, including love and compassion. This does not mean that financial planning and good management are more important than love or compassion, but it does mean that they take more of our attention and focus to do things efficiently, and that is how God wants them done.

Now, would it be better to have the money to feed five thousand people every day or the spiritual authority to multiply a couple of hamburgers into enough food to feed that many? I think we would all choose the latter, and the Lord said that He would not trust us with these **"true riches**—access to the resources of heaven—unless we are faithful with our **"unrighteous mammon" (see Luke 16:11)**. This is why we have a responsibility to be givers and share the material resources we have been blessed with, but let us also see that it is done in a way that actually helps people and really does some good. True goodness is much more than just having good intentions—it is actually healing people, setting them free, and leading them to the Source who alone is the answer to all human needs.

When we recently sent a team to a remote village in Africa to dig wells for them, I was shocked to learn how many thousands of such wells had been dug throughout Africa that were no longer working. Some only worked for a few weeks or months until they became inoperative for the lack of a simple part like a washer. As great as the intentions were for these ministries to supply pure water to these people, without a simple maintenance plan or training the Africans to maintain the wells, huge resources were wasted, and the hope of these villages was turned into a greater disappointment. One of the ways we determined that we could best use our resources for this was to find out where these wells were, fix them (which usually would cost just a fraction of the cost of drilling another well), and put them on a simple inspection and maintenance plan to keep them going.

With all of our compassion, we must start thinking practically, and for a longer term. Africa is experiencing an unemployment rate of 85 percent or more in some regions. They are very eager to learn. Why not train some of them to both drill and maintain these wells? That is, of course, what we are seeking to do, but with all of our compassion and desire to help, we must really help people by being better managers of what we are being entrusted with.

As Christians, we also need to examine where we are putting our charitable gifts. I quit giving to the United Way when they quit giving to the Boy Scouts because of the Boy Scouts' wise and very practical stand against having homosexual scout leaders. We have a responsibility to see that our gifts are used righteously, as well as efficiently.

There has been a tendency for much of the church to swing too far away from social efforts because it does seem that ministries who are given totally to this often succumb to humanistic tendencies and philosophies. In the time ahead, the church must become what most of our buildings are called: "sanctuaries." As I recently told a U.S. senator who called me after Hurricane Katrina, the government is going to run out of resources and not be able to keep up with the problems ahead, but the church that is abiding in the Vine has access to the resources of heaven that can never be exhausted.

The church is going to emerge as the frontline and first defense against all that is coming. We must get ready for this. I am praying now for much greater resources than the federal government has. I know that for the Lord to trust me with them, I must use them to truly do good and to do this efficiently. Let us use every opportunity now to do good, and learn every lesson so that we can do even more good the next time our neighbors need us.

CHAPTER TWENTY-SEVEN

FAITHFULNESS

The next aspect of the fruit of the Spirit is **"faithfulness."** As we have discussed, the characteristics of the Spirit are called **"fruit"** because they must be cultivated and grown. It takes faithfulness, which is faith with endurance, for any of the fruit to be grown. But how is faithfulness grown? This is important for us to understand if we are going to bear any fruit.

Fruit grows on trees, not small plants. A small plant may sprout and produce vegetables in a single season, but a fruit tree takes years to develop before it will bear fruit. This is why we are told it takes **"faith and patience"** to inherit the promises (see Hebrews 6:12). One reason why there is so little true fruit of the Spirit in the body of Christ today is because of the lack of faithfulness demonstrated by endurance over time until fruit is produced.

I hear many complaints about how pastors and leaders tend to interpret faithfulness by how committed the people are to their own vision. This may be true, but this is not necessarily wrong. In fact, to be faithful to someone else's vision is crucial for developing maturity in Christians so that they, too, can bear fruit.

For many years, our ministry has promoted the need for people to know their own purpose and have their own vision, but this vision, if it is real, must fit together with a corporate vision. Also, the more significant the calling that we have, the longer and more difficult the time of serving someone else's vision will usually be before He will free us to pursue our own vision.

This is because we are the branches and He is the Vine. A branch cannot bear fruit without abiding in the Vine so that His life will flow through us. We receive His life by grace, and we are told plainly that **"God is opposed to the proud, but gives grace to the humble" (James 4:6)**. It takes humility to serve someone else's vision. Without humility, we cannot expect His grace.

The greater the purpose that you have, the more difficult you can expect your call to serve someone else's vision to be. Because King David was called not only to be a king, but to establish the throne the Lord Jesus sits upon, the greatest level of humility and faithfulness was required of him. He had to remain faithful serving a king, who not only had drifted from the will of God, but began to oppose the Lord, killing his priests, and even trying to kill David. However, David remained faithful to Saul even after Saul died.

It is an amazing thing to see how King David rewarded those who honored Saul by recovering his body and giving him a proper burial, but he went even further than this. When it was the practice of kings who ascended a throne in those times to kill all of the offspring of any potential rivals, King David did the opposite. He actually honored Saul's offspring, and even let them eat at honored positions at his own table. David remained faithful to Saul even when Saul became unfaithful. By this, King David became one of the greatest examples of godly faithfulness in the Scriptures.

Of course, One who exceeds even David in faithfulness is the Lord Himself. He has remained faithful to man even through all of man's unfaithfulness and opposition. As the primary work that the Lord is doing in us is to conform us to His image, we can, therefore, expect to be called on to remain faithful to those who have been unfaithful to us. How many of us, knowing that our best friends were all going to deny and betray us that very night, deserting us when we needed them the most, would still desire to have one more meal with them, and even wash their feet to demonstrate our commitment to them?

If we react to those who disappoint us or are unfaithful to us, then we are still immature. Everything that the Lord allows in our lives is for the purpose of conforming us to His image, and if we want this to happen, we can expect to have to go through the same things that He did.

Paul the Apostle prayed to be conformed to the image of the Lord's death, and his prayer was answered. He died with all of his faithful friends having likewise scattered from him, and most of the churches he had given his life to serving had already gone into apostasy. Paul probably died wondering if he had really accomplished anything through his life of sacrifice. True sacrifice has a power to bear fruit that actually cannot be destroyed. Paul had probably long ago forgotten about the few letters he had written from prison. However, because Paul lived for eternity instead of the temporary, there was an eternal quality to those letters that made it impossible for them to be destroyed. Those few letters with eternity in their hearts are probably still bearing more fruit for eternal life than all of the efforts of those who are in ministry today. But would they have been remembered if Paul had not been so faithful, even to the end, even unto death? Probably not.

We must resolve that our own faithfulness will not be determined by what others do. We must resolve to remain faithful simply because it is the right thing to do. Even if it looks as if we will be alone, and we cannot see any fruit from it, it is still the right thing to do.

Of course, the ultimate test of faithfulness would probably be in relation to a spouse. Isn't this what the Lord Himself is daily going through with His bride? How many of you would have liked to hear from your spouse-to-be on your wedding day, "Darling, I am going to be totally faithful to you 364 days a year. I only want one day a year to mess around."

James 4:4 says, **"You adulteresses, do you not know that friendship with the world is hostility toward God? Therefore whoever wishes to be a friend of the world makes himself an enemy of God."**

How many of His people have not devoted themselves far more to being joined to and successful in the world than to being joined to Him? Is this true of us? Then we, too, are being unfaithful to the One who in all of creation deserves our faithfulness the most.

If you have a question about whether this is you or not, ask yourself this question: What do I spend most of my time doing and what has most of my attention? Am I more focused on how to get ahead in my job or profession, making more money, or acquiring the things of this world than knowing the Lord, getting closer to Him, and doing His will? If so, then at the very least you have lost your first love, and you are in spiritual adultery with the world.

It is also possible to be more devoted to our church or our ministry than to the Lord Himself. As ministers, we are called to be the friends of the Bridegroom who are helping to prepare the bride for Him, but how many in ministry are really just using the bride to serve themselves and their own ambition? Isn't this the most profane of all unfaithfulness? In this way we are not only unfaithful ourselves, but we are seeking to have the very bride of Christ joined more to us than to Him! By this we are committing adultery with God's own wife!

This is a trap that many in ministry fall into, and they may well deserve the worst judgment on that day. In relation to our being His bride, what husband would want a wife that was so busy serving Him that she had no time for him? What husband would want a wife that loved her job or her house more than she loved him? This, too, is an issue of faithfulness.

Many in ministry are disappointed in the lack of people's faithfulness to our vision when we ourselves are very basically being unfaithful to the Lord, and the people can see it. They will ultimately be as faithful to us as they can see that we are faithful to Him.

Why do we so easily desert Him for that which has no true satisfaction? For the last three years, Jack Deere and I have scheduled an around-the-world ministry trip each summer to try and serve as many countries as we could in the few weeks that we have. Each year, Jack is usually in the middle of some study that we spend time talking about, while sharing dozens of hours in airports and on airplanes. On our last trip, Jack found a study on "happiness." The findings of this study were not only very interesting— they were quite surprising. The study found that the amount of material possessions, or the lack of them, actually had no real bearing on a person's happiness.

I pondered this quite a bit on that trip, especially in Africa, where it seemed the majority of the population had so little. Then, as if to emphasize this, while we were in Johannesburg, South Africa, my wife and daughters visited the famous township of Soweto. They had a wonderful guide who took them to Nelson Mandela's house and to the other historic sites of this shanty town where the revolution in South Africa had begun. When he was showing them the typical house, which was usually two rooms, one of them being the kitchen where there was an open fire and where all of the children usually slept, a friend who was on the tour remarked how sorry he was for them to have to grow up in these conditions. The guide was surprised by this comment, saying that they should not be sorry for this because they had a very happy family, and the memories of his childhood were not of deprivation, but of all the good times they had together.

I grew up in a very unhappy family, with difficult and confusing problems, one of which was continued and serious financial stress. Because of that I have been driven to do better for my own family. However, three times we have had to move from "dream homes" to much smaller and more difficult conditions, and every time I have witnessed the barometer of our family's happiness go up instead of down, and often quite dramatically.

Our over-devotion to materialism is a trap and a deception that is robbing us of true life. So how is it that we could be more faithful to that vision than to the Son of God? It is a righteous thing to want to provide well for your family, but we must guard against this becoming an idol that eclipses our devotion to the Lord. When it does, the fruit will be bad for ourselves and those we are doing it for.

We were all created to have fellowship with God, and there is never going to be anything else more interesting or fulfilling than this. As stated, *the main thing in our lives is to keep the main thing the main thing.* How is it that we are so easily distracted from this? Unfaithfulness.

The Lord develops faithfulness within us in many ways. One primary way is by having us devote ourselves to the visions and purposes of others. This is what all true ministry is: servanthood. This is quite a lost art in ministry today, but it will be recovered. When it is, we will discover that there is really nothing as fulfilling as serving the Lord and helping others succeed in their purpose. It is hard for the immature to see this, but this is actually the path for us to succeed in our own purpose.

Paul the Apostle lamented that there were many teachers, but not many fathers (see I Corinthians 4:15). That is true. A true father will receive far more satisfaction out of seeing his children succeed than from his own success. This is why the true measure of an authentic New Testament ministry is for one to reproduce their ministry in others and have them succeed. If it was the nature of God to empty Himself of all His glory and lower Himself to become a man to serve the very ones who had rejected Him, then we who were made in His image will also do this.

The Lord requires the immature to go through a time of serving someone else's vision before He will let them pursue their own. If we are on the path of true ministry, our main devotion will not be to get others to support our vision as much as we will be devoted to helping those entrusted to our care be prepared and released into their own purpose. True ministry is never just faithfulness to our own vision, but serving others. In the Lord, the only way to fulfill our own vision is to serve Him and serve His people—servanthood. True faithfulness to the Lord is just as He stated in Matthew 16:24-26:

> **Then Jesus said to His disciples, "If anyone wishes to come after Me, let him deny himself, and take up his cross, and follow Me.**

> **"For whoever wishes to save his life shall lose it; but whoever loses his life for My sake shall find it.**

> **"For what will a man be profited, if he gains the whole world, and forfeits his soul? Or what will a man give in exchange for his soul?"**

Faithfulness to someone else requires the laying aside of our own self-centeredness, even the fulfilling of "our ministry," and giving ourselves to the purpose of another. The Lord has made us so that this is the only way we can truly find our own purpose and fulfillment. There is no greater bondage than self-centeredness, and no greater freedom than being the Lord's slave. However, the truly faithful will remain steadfast when it becomes hard, regardless of how much time it takes. True faithfulness will see the job through to completion.

Every leader learns fast that it is quite easy to get people motivated to start a job, but there will not be many who will see it through the hard work to completion. The resurrected Lord told five hundred people to go back to Jerusalem to wait for the promise of the Holy Spirit, but after just twelve days there were only one hundred twenty still there. The Lord knew this would happen. He often causes things to take longer than we would like to thin out the crowds, getting rid of the unfaithful, because anything of true significance must be built on faithful people. This is why He requires that we not only have faith, but also patience to inherit the promises.

True Christian maturity requires that we learn faithfulness to a corporate vision, something that originated in the heart of someone else, which may or may not be the main thing on our hearts, but this is needed before we can expect others to be committed to our vision. Few visions and purposes of the Lord can be accomplished by just one person, so it does require a joining together of others to accomplish them. However, the basis of our faithfulness must be to the Lord Himself above all other things, keeping Him as our first love. That is the basis of all true faithfulness.

One of the primary areas which demonstrates faithfulness is our financial giving. Even most

Christians have a negative reaction to this, but it is true and biblical. This is the reason why the Lord Himself was watching those who were giving in the temple. Jesus, being the true representative of the Father, demonstrated that this was something important to the Father. This is because where a person's treasure is, there will his heart be also.

When I was once inquiring of the Lord about how to know who to add to our staff for a position, the Lord said that I should look at their record of giving to see if their hearts were really with us. Since then I have concluded that this probably is truly the best barometer of a person's faithfulness. If their hearts really are with the Lord, they will put their treasure into His work. If their hearts are with you in what you are doing for Him, they will invest there. If they will not put their treasure there, then you can be sure their heart is not really there either.

The very thought of this will cause a strong reaction in some, but those are the ones whom you will not be able to count on because they are the ones who will demand the most and give the least. When difficulties come, they will be the first to become disgruntled, and the fastest to desert. In my observations, this has been true every time. Money is usually the ultimate idol—what we put our trust in even above the Lord. Where a person puts his treasure will be where his heart really is. That is why, if we are true shepherds, we have a basic responsibility to teach those entrusted to our care financial faithfulness, too.

CHAPTER TWENTY-EIGHT

GENTLENESS

The next aspect of the fruit of the Spirit is **"gentleness."** This is defined as being "mild, kind," or "not being rough, violent, harsh or severe." Some people may be born with a natural, gentle demeanor, but the fruit of the Spirit that is gentleness is to conduct ourselves with sensitivity and consideration for others.

Gentleness is a characteristic that enables others to feel that they can get close to you and be safe. If you are wondering why it seems that people do not want to be close to you, a lack of this characteristic of the Spirit could be the problem. Those who are harsh will repel others like a thorny bush. The more gentle you are, the closer people will usually feel they can get to you.

In Psalm 18:35 King David writes, **"You have also given me the shield of Your salvation; Your right hand has held me up. Your gentleness has made me great"** (NKJV). David, one of the greatest warriors in the Old Testament said that it was the Lord's gentleness that made him great. How is this? Gentleness has been the presumed nature of nobility because it is the basis for a truly noble character, which is why they are called "gentlemen" or "gentlewomen." To be gentle not only demonstrates caring for others, but also demonstrates the wisdom of restraint and self-control.

This is why it is also a very basic apostolic characteristic, as we read in such Scriptures as II Corinthians 10:1, **"Now I, Paul, myself am pleading with you by the meekness and gentleness of Christ..."** (NKJV). Artists have portrayed this gentleness of Christ by Him carrying a lamb or surrounded by children, and though it is amazing to think of the Creator of the universe like this, it is accurate. God is a very gentle Person. The Holy Spirit is even portrayed as a dove, possibly the most gentle and sensitive of birds.

Therefore, gentleness is a characteristic of the truly spiritual, just as Paul implied in Galatians 6:1, **"Brethren, if a man is overtaken in any trespass, you who are spiritual restore such a one in a spirit of gentleness, considering yourself lest you also be tempted"** (NKJV), Redemption and restoration are the primary business of the Lord on this earth, and gentleness is essential for all who are involved in His work.

I confess to being a "type A" personality. I am a goal-oriented builder. I like to get things done, and see the results. However, this does, at times, cause me to care more about a project than the people that the project is for. In the drive to get the project done for the people, I can easily hurt the people I am doing it for without even realizing it.

When we purchased the Heritage Grand Hotel and Conference Center that was formerly called PTL, or Heritage USA, it looked so devastated and run-down that we were able to purchase it for the value of the land, subtracting the cost of tearing down all of the buildings and removing the rubble. It simply looked too run-down to restore. However, in just a few weeks we had a certificate of occupancy and were able to hold church services there for our congregation. In a few more months, we had nearly 20 percent of the rooms restored and usable. In a year to eighteen months, we expect to have the job completed, with the entire facility restored to "like new" or better. This is being done by a team who are all "just get it done" types. When any of this team is put in a situation, in just a short time, something will get done. I like and feel most comfortable around those types, but I do not think "gentleness" would be the first thing anyone would think of in relation to any of us. However, we need to be, and I consider this one of our greatest challenges.

So how do we reconcile this with the ultimate purpose of God to "restore all things"? First, we have to always keep in mind that a single soul is far more valuable than all buildings, and that our main job in the ministry is building people, not things. People are far more fragile than all of this steel and lumber. You would not want to see a surgeon come in with a tool kit of hammers and chainsaws! A person's soul is even more fragile than his or her body is. We may need a sledgehammer when remodeling a building, but not when trying to help renew a person. This is why Paul wrote in II Timothy 2:24-25, **"And the Lord's bond-servant must not be quarrelsome, but be kind to all, able to teach, patient when wronged, with gentleness correcting those who are in opposition, if perhaps God may grant them repentance leading to the knowledge of the truth."**

Think about this: The bond-servant of the Lord **"must not be quarrelsome."** When we become harsh in our arguments in defense of the gospel, we actually depart from the nature of the Spirit of truth, who can alone penetrate the veil of deception and lead someone to the truth. There is a certain dignity with which the King always conducts Himself, which is also required of His representatives. Even when correcting those who are in opposition to the gospel, we must be gentle. The reason for this is explained in Proverbs 15:1-2, **"A gentle answer turns away wrath, but a harsh word stirs up anger. The tongue of the wise makes knowledge acceptable, but the mouth of fools spouts folly."**

As Paul also wrote in Ephesians 4:1-3, **"I, therefore, the prisoner of the Lord, beseech you to walk worthy of the calling with which you were called, with all lowliness and gentleness, with longsuffering, bearing with one another in love, endeavoring to keep the unity of the Spirit in the bond of peace"** (NKJV). Here we see that to walk in a manner worthy of our calling requires gentleness.

Colossians 3:12-13 states, **"And so, as those who have been chosen of God, holy and beloved, put on a heart of compassion, kindness, humility, gentleness and patience; bearing with one another, and forgiving each other, whoever has a complaint against anyone; just as the Lord forgave you, so also should you."** Compassion, kindness, humility, gentleness, and patience are all linked together, and this is a heart that we are to **"put on."** How do we do that?

We put on our clothes every day before meeting other people. Mature, considerate people consider whom they are meeting and dress appropriately. To not do so is to show disrespect for the person you are meeting with. This is so important to the Lord that in Matthew 22, the Lord taught that if someone came to a wedding feast not dressed appropriately, they would be thrown into the outer darkness. Certainly, He did not mean this just for weddings, but the principle is to come to an occasion dressed appropriately as a basic show of respect for those who invited you. If this is true of our clothes, how much more should it be true of our behavior?

In this way, we should consider the people whom we are meeting and put on the appropriate demeanor, and gentleness is always appropriate. Once, when I was walking near Buckingham Palace in London, I felt the Lord ask me what I would do if I met the Queen. Thinking that this was about to happen, I thought of all the protocol I knew, which was not much, so I simply thought that I would treat her with as much respect as I knew how. Then I felt the Lord say that His church is His bride, the true queen, and that I should, likewise, always treat her with the utmost respect whenever I address her. Even if some correction had to be brought to a queen, we would do it with the respect and dignity that her place requires. We should consider this even more when we bring correction to a church.

Because all people were made in the image of God, they are, therefore, worthy of being treated with dignity and respect, even if they have lost that for themselves. To do so can help raise such people out of the pit they have fallen into. To treat someone with gentleness is a very basic expression of respect.

Even Peter, the rugged former fisherman wrote, **"but sanctify Christ as Lord in your hearts, always being ready to make a defense to everyone who asks you to give an account for the hope that is in you, yet with gentleness and reverence" (I Peter 3:15).**

This is why we are told in James 3:13, **"Who among you is wise and understanding? Let him show by his good behavior his deeds in the gentleness of wisdom."** Gentleness is an unmistakable quality of true wisdom that comes from above.

After reciting the traps laid for those who pursue earthly riches, Paul concludes his exhortation in I Timothy 6:11-12, **"But flee from these things, you man of God; and pursue righteousness, godliness, faith, love, perseverance and gentleness. Fight the** good fight of faith; take hold of the eternal life to which you were called...." Therefore, gentleness should be one of our pursuits, so that we might walk in a manner worthy of our calling, in the wisdom that comes from above.

CHAPTER TWENTY-NINE

SELF-CONTROL

It is interesting that the last characteristic of the fruit of the Spirit listed is **"self-control."** These are the fruit of the Spirit, from seeds sown and cultivated by the Spirit, but with our help. To walk in them, we are going to have to learn to control ourselves. This is something the Spirit will not do because it would be a violation of who we were created to be.

Many Christians, in seeking to become submitted to the Holy Spirit or to eschew glory for anything that is accomplished through them spiritually, often say such things as "That was not me—that was the Lord." This may be a noble attempt to not take glory for things accomplished by the Lord, but this reveals a fundamental misunderstanding of how the Spirit actually does His work. Even worse, this often comes across to others as something between supreme arrogance and ridiculous.

I once saw a professional golfer make a shot which did seem borderline miraculous, but when he claimed in an interview, "That wasn't me—that was the Lord," I could not help but think, if the Lord was operating through his golf game like that, did the Lord get that double bogey, too? In fact, wouldn't the Lord get a hole in one on every shot?

My point is, though there are obvious miracles which have nothing to do with our power or ability, the Lord works through people as they pray for someone. It is a basic misunderstanding of the way the Spirit operates to think that man is not involved at all in His works. We are called "His body" because He works with us and through us. This is why self-control is a fruit of the Spirit. It is "self" control, and we must be involved, but He works with us.

When children are very young, they must be told what to do or not to do almost continually. However, as they mature you expect them to understand and use their own wisdom more and more to make such decisions. Parents rejoice when children start using their own good judgment and do not have to ask about every little thing. The Lord is the same with us. Having to be continually led by the Lord in every detail is not a sign of spiritual maturity, but immaturity.

As we mature, we do not need the leading of the Spirit in every little thing because our minds have been renewed and we have grown in wisdom and discernment. This is why the apostles were not led around by the hand, but *sent* by the Spirit. They were mature enough to make decisions, and only received prophetic revelation for direction when the Lord wanted to change their course or send them to a place they were not intending to go. That is the way the spiritually mature operate, using their own judgment, but always being open for the Lord to change or modify a decision or direction.

That may sound unspiritual to some, but the other is actually pseudo-spiritual, or at the least very immature. God does His work on the earth through men, and it is the devil that tries to make men into mere puppets. This is why such immature people also tend to blame all of their mistakes on the devil instead of just confessing them. God does not forgive excuses—He forgives sin that is confessed.

To have self-control is obviously to be in control of ourselves. This implies not letting our emotions control us, but rather controlling our emotions. It also means that we do not allow external things to control our behavior. Of course, this is an essential character-istic of any who are going to walk in the Spirit and have the fruit of the Spirit. We should have peace in the midst of any conflict or chaos. We should have faith where there is fear and love where there is hatred. For this we must be controlled from our inner man, and not from any outside source.

For people to have self-control, true conviction of sin is required, which can also be a primary factor in people coming under the conviction of the Holy Spirit, as we read in Acts 24:24-25, **"But some days later, Felix arrived with Drusilla, his wife who was a Jewess, and sent for Paul, and heard him speak about** faith in Christ Jesus. And as he was discussing righteousness, self-control and the judgment to come, Felix became frightened and said, 'Go away for the present, and when I find time, I will summon you.'"

It is self-control that compels us to the discipline which is required for a mature and victorious Christian life, just as we are told in I Corinthians 9:24-27, "Do you not know that those who run in a race all run, but only one receives the prize? Run in such a way that you may win. And everyone who competes in the games exercises self-control in all things. They then do it to receive a perishable wreath, but we an imperishable. Therefore I run in such a way, as not without aim; I box in such a way, as not beating the air; but I buffet my body and make it my slave, lest possibly, after I have preached to others, I myself should be disqualified."

In this, we see that a lack of self-control can cause us to lose our reward, canceling out the good that we may do. How many ministries, after years of faithfulness and endurance through the various trials that all ministries go through to grow, unravel because of a single indiscretion of the leader? Hasn't this also been the case in many political campaigns as well? As Paul uses the metaphor of running a race, great runners do not just run to the finish line, but set their goal past it so that they run at full speed through the finish line. We must do the same so we, too, will not be in danger of being disqualified.

In II Timothy 3:1-5, we read about what the condition of people in the last days will be: **"But realize this, that in the last days difficult times will come. For men will be lovers of self, lovers of money, boastful, arrogant, revilers, disobedient to parents, ungrateful, unholy, unloving, irreconcilable, malicious gossips,** *without self-control,* **brutal, haters of good, treacherous, reckless, conceited, lovers of pleasure rather than lovers of God; holding to a form of godliness, although they have denied its power; and avoid such men as these."** Those who are without self-control will be controlled by the evil one, who will always seize that opportunity.

On the other hand, God will not dominate anyone, but will help them to control themselves. This is why we are told in II Peter 1:5-7 that **"self-control"** is such an integral step in spiritual maturity:

> **Now for this very reason also, applying all diligence, in your faith supply moral excellence, and in your moral excellence, knowledge;**

> **and in your knowledge, self-control, and in your self-control, perseverance, and in your perseverance, godliness;**

> **and in your godliness, brotherly kindness, and in your brotherly kindness,** [Christian] **love.**

Self-control is listed as the last characteristic of the fruit of the Spirit, but it is by no means the least important. Self-control is essential if we are going to exhibit any of these characteristics with consistency and, therefore, abide in the Holy Spirit.

CHAPTER THIRTY

SUMMARY

We have just studied two of the most important issues in any Christian's life—the works of the flesh and the fruit of the Spirit. If the works of the flesh are not cut off, as we are told in Galatians 5:21, **"...those who practice such things shall not inherit the kingdom of God."** It is that serious. If any of those things listed as works of the flesh continue to have a place in our lives, a top priority must be to cut them off.

However, the Christian life is not just refusing to do what is evil, but it is a life of doing good— walking in the fruit of the Spirit. As we are told in Ephesians 4:14-16:

> **As a result, we are no longer to be children, tossed here and there by waves, and carried about by every wind of doctrine, by the trickery of men, by craftiness in deceitful scheming;**

> **but speaking the truth in love, we are to grow up in all aspects into Him, who is the head, even Christ,**

from whom the whole body, being fitted and held together by that which every joint supplies, according to the proper working of each individual part, causes the growth of the body for the building up of itself in love.

If we are growing up "in all aspects into Him," the fruit of the Spirit will be our nature. It is upon this foundation that the gifts of the Spirit operate. This does not mean that we should grow in the fruit of the Spirit just so we can be trusted with the power of the Spirit. It is true that we can be trusted with more power when we are abiding in Him and, therefore, have the fruit of the Spirit, but our primary calling is what we are called to be, not just what we are called to do. The fruit is the goal.

Growing in the fruit of the Spirit is the foundation of a godly life, and it is the ultimate goal as well. This is why He said that His disciples would be known by their love, not just their acts (see John 13:35). The primary goal of our lives should be to love God. The next greatest goal is to love others. Therefore, let us have the resolve to love God more each day and love one another more. This is the essence of our purpose for being.

True in nature is that once a living thing stops growing, it starts the process of dying. You are called to never die. We begin eternity with a life that is ever-growing. That life is evidenced by an increasing harvest of the fruit of the Spirit. Never stop growing! What you do may be noteworthy, but what you become will last forever.

Strategic Water

MST Mission II: ZAO Life Project

Every 8 seconds a child dies from water related diseases. We are helping to solve the problem with natural and spiritual water for Africa.

*W*e invite you to partner with us to help save a continent both physically and spiritually. Africa will know the power and love of our God. MST is our **MorningStar Strategic Team**, our fellowship of partners who give monthly and help support the missions of MorningStar, like ZAO. There is no minimum contribution amount.

Support Strategic Missions.
Join the Team.

For more information or to join MST:

- Call us at 1-800-542-0278

- Visit us online at
  MST.MorningStarMinistries.org

- Write to us at 375 Star Light Drive,
  Fort Mill, SC 29715

MST
MorningStar Strategic Team
Partners Supporting Missions